NAZIK

P9-APC-671

LIFE ON EARTH
FIRST LIFE

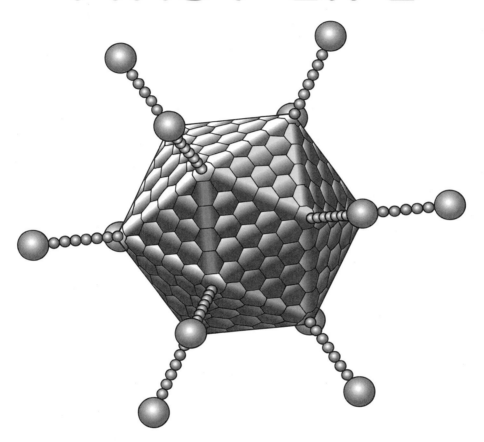

THE DIAGRAM GROUP

Facts On File, Inc.

Life On Earth: First Life

Written, edited, and produced by Diagram Visual Information Ltd

Editorial director:	Denis Kennedy
Editors:	Bender Richardson White, Gordon Lee
Contributor:	Gerard E. Cheshire
Indexer:	Martin Hargreaves
Art director:	Roger Kohn
Senior designer:	Lee Lawrence
Designers:	Anthony Atherton, Christian Owens
Illustrators:	Julian Baker, Pavel Kostal, Kathleen McDougall, Sean Milne, Jack Morris, Coral Mula, Graham Rosewarne
Picture researcher:	Neil McKenna

Facts On File, Inc.
132 West 31st Street
New York NY 10001

For Library of Congress Cataloging-in-Publication Data, please contact Facts On File, Inc.
  ISBN 0-8160-5046-5

Facts On File books are available at special discounts when purchased in bulk quantities for businesses, associations, institutions, or sales promotions. Please call our Special Sales Department in New York at 212/967-8800 or 800/322-8755.

You can find Facts On File on the World Wide Web at: http://www.factsonfile.com

Printed in the United States of America

EB Diagram   10   9   8   7   6   5   4   3   2   1

This book is printed on acid-free paper.

Contents

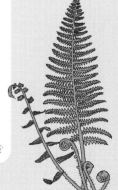

Introduction

THIS BOOK is a concise, illustrated guide to the way life first appeared on Earth, and how it developed and diversified into the vast range of plants and animals now in existence. The story has taken hundreds of millions of years, and the variety of life-forms has been so wide that it would be impossible to cover everything in detail. Instead, the subject is dealt with in clear steps and topics so that an overall understanding can gradually be acquired. Texts, explanatory diagrams, illustrations, captions, and feature boxes combine to help readers grasp important information. A glossary clarifies the more difficult scientific terms for younger students, while a list of websites provides links to other relevant sources of additional information.

Chapter 1, *Cells as Building Blocks*, discusses the ways in which scientists think life first appeared on the Earth, and how it evolved into single-celled organisms equipped with DNA in their nuclei.

Chapter 2, *The Variety of Life*, covers the extraordinary journey that saw single-celled organisms evolve into multicelled plants and invertebrate animals that colonized the Earth's oceans, lands, freshwater, and skies.

Chapter 3, *The Basis of Evolution*, explains how evolution works, in terms of both natural selection and genetics. The ways in which scientists categorize species, and the pioneers of evolutionary biology are also introduced.

Chapter 4, *Simple and Soft-bodied*, is a description of the most primitive invertebrates, which survived perfectly well without skeletons, either inside or outside of their bodies.

Chapter 5, *Simple, but with Body Armor*, looks at the ways in which invertebrates evolved to include first external, then internal skeletons as the demands on their designs rose with competition between species.

Chapter 6, *Body Systems*, examines the workings of invertebrate animals, such as means of locomotion, methods of communication, reproductive strategies, and the ways in which species develop from larval forms into adults.

Chapter 7, *Detection and Response*, scrutinizes the sensory workings of invertebrates. The fundamental sensory organs are described, with the coordination of nervous systems and brains that enabled them to survive.

First Life is one of six titles in the Life On Earth series that looks at the evolution and diversity of our planet, its features, and living things.

The series features all life-forms, from bacteria and algae to trees and mammals. It also highlights the infinite variety of adaptations and strategies for survival among living things, and describes different habitats, how they evolved, and the communities of creatures that inhabit them. Individual chapters discuss the characteristics of specific taxonomic groups of living things, or types of landscape or planetary features.

Life On Earth has been written by natural history experts, and is generously illustrated with line drawings, labeled diagrams, and maps. The series provides students with a solid, necessary foundation for their future studies in science.

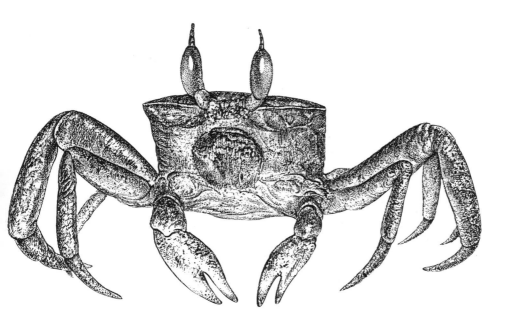

Exactly how life on Earth began has been a mystery ever since people first realized there might be a scientific explanation.

THE FIRST SCIENTIST to make any significant headway into how life began on the Earth was the American biological chemist Stanley Miller. In 1953 he conducted an important experiment based on some educated guesswork. He calculated what the Earth's atmosphere might have been like before life began, and then recreated it in his laboratory. He mixed ammonia, hydrogen, and methane gases together in a chamber with water vapor. At the time, these were thought to have been the early atmosphere's components. He then used electricity to simulate a lightning storm to see what effect it might have on the mixture. To the world's amazement Miller's experiment yielded amino acid molecules, which were known to be the basic building blocks of the proteins that are found in all living organisms.

Pioneer
Stanley Miller, a biological chemist, opened the way to our understanding the genesis of life.

Following Miller's discovery, another American scientist, Sidney Fox, showed that, under the right conditions, amino acids will link together to form simple proteinlike molecules called proteinoids.

Man-made cells
These cell-like structures are the closest science has come to creating life from scratch.

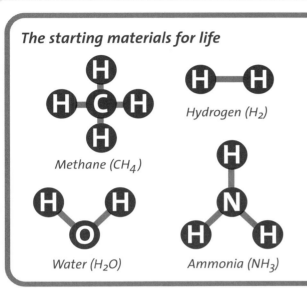

The starting materials for life

Methane (CH$_4$)

Hydrogen (H$_2$)

Water (H$_2$O)

Ammonia (NH$_3$)

These are inclined to congregate into cell-like spheres with the capacity to grow and bring about simple chemical reactions.

Since the work done by Miller and Fox, there has been slow progress in this field of biological chemistry. No one can claim to have created life, but their work has shown that life is likely to have begun in a similar way. There may have been an element of chance, involving a large number of natural experiments, until a simple organism happened to conjure itself from the primal ooze. Or it may be that the conditions required are very specific and too complicated to achieve in a laboratory. What we do know about all life on the Earth is that it seems to have evolved from a single source, which suggests that there is just one way for it to happen.

DID YOU KNOW?
All organisms on the Earth are described as "carbon-based" life-forms. This means that the molecules from which they are physically constructed contain carbon compounds, or organic compounds, as they are otherwise known. Carbon atoms readily combine with atoms of hydrogen, oxygen, and nitrogen to form amino acids. There are about twenty amino acids, and from these an infinite variety of organic compounds can be created.

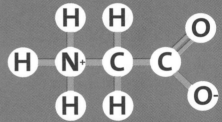

Glycine (gly)
This is a common amino acid.

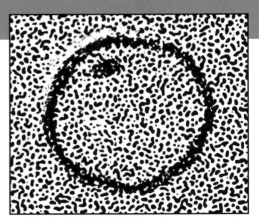

Fossilized single-celled alga
This is a simple carbon-based life-form from a billion years ago.

© DIAGRAM

When the first organisms appeared on the Earth, it was a very different place. Stanley Miller's experiment (see page 6) showed that the Earth's atmosphere lacked any oxygen, which meant that early organisms had to rely on utilizing simple organic molecules for their fundamental life process.

ANCIENT ORGANISMS STILL EXIST and are collectively known as Archaea. After living on the Earth for many millions of years, they gave rise to photosynthetic bacteria, which produced oxygen as a waste product of their chemistry. This was the cue for new organisms, called cyanobacteria, or blue-green algae, to evolve.

The next stage in the evolution of life was the development of the cell nucleus, which contains all of the information to reproduce more complex organisms. This information is stored in the form of

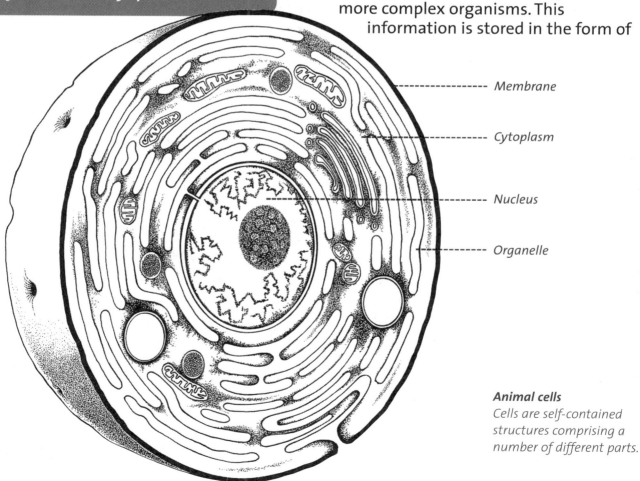

Membrane

Cytoplasm

Nucleus

Organelle

Animal cells
Cells are self-contained structures comprising a number of different parts.

long molecules called DNA (deoxyribonucleic acid). In addition to the nucleus, organisms began to develop simple organlike structures for different purposes, called organelles. With the nucleus and organelles in place, the first advanced, single-celled organism existed, with the potential for evolving into an infinite variety of life-forms. Before long, single-celled organisms began to collaborate by joining together. This meant that they could specialize at different things but share the benefits. Inevitably they became so dependent on each other that they became forever joined as multicelled organisms. These multicelled organisms could then grow larger by multiplying cells, and begin to use specialized cells for different parts of their bodies or structures.

IT'S A FACT
Some scientists group cyanobacteria and bacteria together in a domain called Prokaryotes (meaning "before nucleus"). The domain to which all plants and animals belong is called Eukaryotes ("good nucleus"). The most basic eukaryotes are single-celled organisms, but they still possess all of the components that are found in the cells of multicelled organisms.

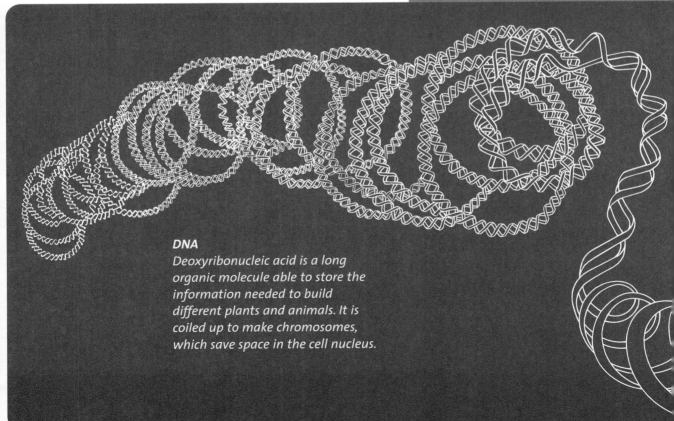

DNA
Deoxyribonucleic acid is a long organic molecule able to store the information needed to build different plants and animals. It is coiled up to make chromosomes, which save space in the cell nucleus.

The earliest life-forms are grouped together in the Prokaryotes domain. "Prokaryote" means "before nucleus" in Greek. There are two types of prokaryote: bacteria and Archaea. They are all single-celled and so small that they are described as microorganisms (microscopic organisms).

BACTERIA ARE very simple organisms, some of which produce their energy by the process known as respiration and others, the cyanobacteria, by photosynthesis. Archaea are similar to bacteria in appearance, but their molecules are organized in a different way. It is thought that Archaea may represent the link between prokaryotes and the group that contains all other plants, fungi, and animals—the Eukaryotes domain. Cyanobacteria are otherwise known as blue-green algae, because of their color when they grow together in their millions. Their greenish color is the chlorophyll they use for photosynthesis, just like most other plants. Cyanobacteria grow in water with very low levels of oxygen, but plenty of carbon dioxide.

Cyanobacteria

Membrane

DNA bundle

Cytoplasm

Chlorophyll

These single-celled, plantlike organisms are also known as blue-green algae due to their "cyan" color.

Bacterium

Membrane

DNA bundle

Cytoplasm

Ribosome

Typical bacteria
These single-celled, animal-like organisms are more numerous and widespread than other forms of life.

Coccus

Types of bacteria
Bacteria are generally spherical, oval, rod-shaped, or spiral-shaped. They have a common simple internal structure and a cell wall that is usually rigid.

IT'S A FACT
Bacteria of the genus *Bacillus* cause disease in animals. They are called bacilli and have a typically rodlike shape when viewed under a microscope. One type causes anthrax (*Bacillus anthracis*). Other bacterial diseases include botulism (*Clostridium botulinum*), listeriosis (*Listeria monocytogenes*), and tuberculosis (*Mycobacterium tuberculosis*).

Bacillus

Spirillus

When conditions are favorable they multiply to such an extent that they form a green mat over the surface of the water, which is called algal bloom. Animal-like bacteria are far more widespread than cyanobacteria. They live everywhere—in water, on land, in air, on other organisms, inside other organisms, and on dead organisms.

Different types of bacteria might be described as either harmful or beneficial depending on their lifestyle. For example, some bacteria cause disease, but other bacteria help animals to digest their food. Bacteria are also very important in the ecosystem, because they decompose dead plants and animals, returning their nutrients to the environment. Archaea are common in lakes, seas, and oceans, and occur in odd places such as undersea vents, hot springs and in salt pans. They may be the most widespread organisms on the Earth.

© DIAGRAM

Prokaryotes all possess DNA but it is not organized into proper nuclei. The first and only organisms to have a proper nucleus were the eukaryotes.

A LL PLANTS AND ANIMALS are eukaryotes, but they evolved from simple, single-celled organisms. The word "eukaryote" means "good kernel" in Greek, or "true nucleus". Having a nucleus marked a key development in evolution because it is a neat package of DNA that can duplicate an organism exactly. This meant that organisms could become more complex but still make accurate copies of themselves. This ability allowed eukaryotes to become highly adapted to their surroundings, and to diversify in an almost infinite number of ways.

Single-celled eukaryotes had an obvious problem. There was only so far they could go with just one cell in terms of size and adaptability. The evolutionary hurdle was overcome as many single-celled eukaryotes combined together to form the first multicelled organisms. By doing so eukaryotes could grow bigger and begin to use different cells for specific purposes. This enabled an infinite variety of life-forms, and in this way, was the perfect means by which evolution could take place.

Ameba
This is one of the simplest eukaryotes. Being single-celled and animal-like, it is classed as a protozoan, or "protist."

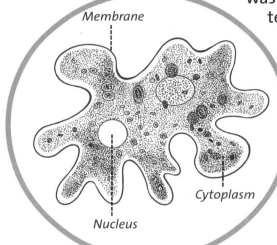

Membrane

Cytoplasm

Nucleus

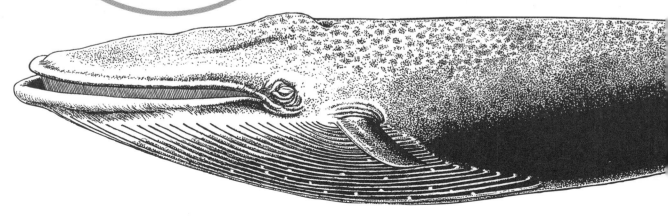

In simple terms, all multicelled organisms are actually colonies of single-celled organisms working together for the greater good of the whole. This includes humans and all other animals or plants. Individual cells are still self-sufficient, but they are sensitive to, and interact with, others. As if to illustrate this point, there are primitive animals whose cells can behave independently. If certain hydra, sponge, and worm species are chopped into pieces, the cells from each piece reform or regenerate into a number of smaller individuals.

STRANGE BUT TRUE
Eukaryotes range in size from single-celled microorganisms to whales and trees. In theory, eukaryotes can grow to any size by adding more cells. However, there are environmental factors that prevent this. Food supply is one factor, as it takes nutrition and energy to build more cells and keep the whole organism alive. There are also physical factors determining whether an organism can support itself.

Giant redwood
This tree is as tall as an organism can grow on land without collapsing under its own weight.

This animal is as large as it is because it uses water to support its body structure.

© DIAGRAM

Early in evolution, a group of suborganisms appeared. These suborganisms are alive, but can only live inside the cells of other organisms. They are the viruses, prions, and virinos.

VIRUSES ARE nothing more than nucleic acid molecules surrounded by protein coatings. As such, their genetic codes are very simple, and they have no means of running their own life processes: they rely on the cells of other organisms to supply them with the food and conditions they need to live and reproduce. They are extremely small and can multiply in their thousands within a host cell. They then break out and invade more cells.

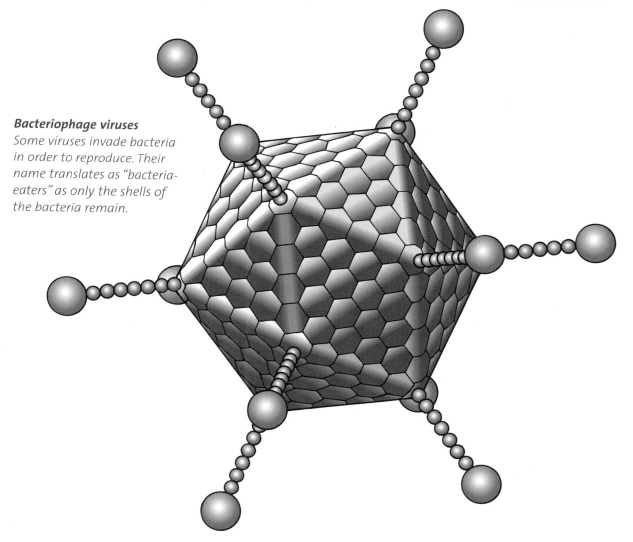

Bacteriophage viruses
Some viruses invade bacteria in order to reproduce. Their name translates as "bacteria-eaters" as only the shells of the bacteria remain.

When this happens, it is described as a viral infection, and is expressed in the host organism as disease. Viral diseases in humans can range from the common cold to AIDS (acquired immunodeficiency syndrome). An interesting characteristic of viruses is that they cannot be removed from the body once infected, as is the case with bacteria by using antibiotics. Even when the symptoms of a disease have gone away, the virus is still present, but lying dormant.

Prions are even simpler than viruses. They are single protein particles that happen to be able to multiply within host organisms in a viruslike manner. Being so simple, prions are very difficult to destroy, and they can cause serious diseases of the nervous system. The term virino is the name for the viruslike structures that prions become once they are established within the cells of a host. Prions and virinos are not fully understood because they work on such a small scale that it is extremely difficult to make scientific observations, even with high-powered microscopes.

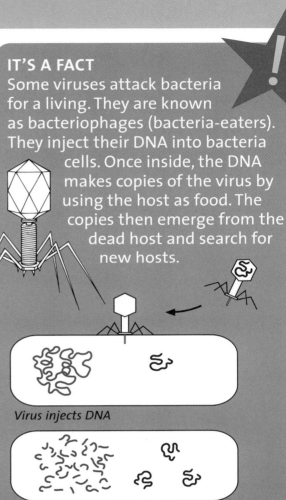

IT'S A FACT
Some viruses attack bacteria for a living. They are known as bacteriophages (bacteria-eaters). They inject their DNA into bacteria cells. Once inside, the DNA makes copies of the virus by using the host as food. The copies then emerge from the dead host and search for new hosts.

Virus injects DNA

Viral DNA breaks down cellular DNA

New viruses are formed using the cellular DNA

New viruses break down a weakened wall and each goes in search of new bacteria

© DIAGRAM

Enter the kingdoms

Eukaryotic organisms are divided into two kingdoms: Plantae (the plant kingdom) and Animalia (the animal kingdom).

THERE ARE SOME ORGANISMS that share plant and animal characteristics, so the distinction between the two is not always clear. Nevertheless, there are certain typical differences between the two. The most obvious is probably that animals can move quickly in response to stimuli, whereas plants cannot. This is because animals possess specialized sense organs, muscles, and nervous systems for this purpose. Another important difference is that animals feed on organic matter and support life by respiration, while plants feed on inorganic matter and support life by photosynthesis. In addition to these differences, animals grow to a set body plan, and most of their cells have

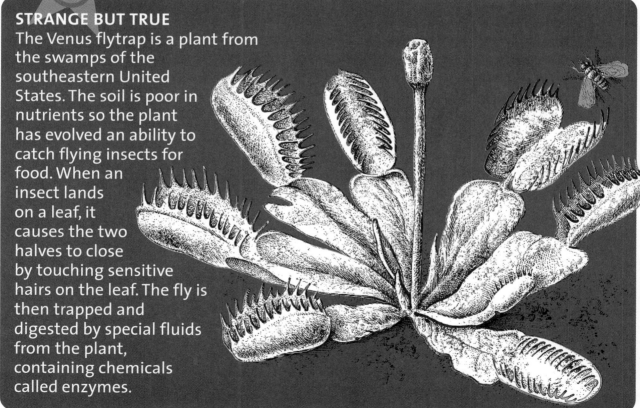

STRANGE BUT TRUE
The Venus flytrap is a plant from the swamps of the southeastern United States. The soil is poor in nutrients so the plant has evolved an ability to catch flying insects for food. When an insect lands on a leaf, it causes the two halves to close by touching sensitive hairs on the leaf. The fly is then trapped and digested by special fluids from the plant, containing chemicals called enzymes.

soft walls for flexibility. Plants have a body plan but more flexible forms, and most of their cell walls are rigid, having little requirement for flexibility.

Some organisms confuse the rules. There is a group of protozoans (single-celled organisms), called phytoflagellates, which possess chlorophyll. This means they can photosynthesize food like plants. But they can move and respond to stimuli as if they were animals.

In the plant kingdom there are species that eat organic food, in the form of insects, in a manner similar to animals. They are fittingly called carnivorous plants and include pitcher plants, sundews and the Venus flytrap. In addition to their carnivorous feeding habits, the leaves of some of these plants can move quickly in response to the stimulus of their prey, making them even more animal-like. There are other animals that live out their lives in a plantlike manner. Sponges, corals, and moss animals can look like plants because they remain stationary, and grow by branching outward as though they might be bushes without leaves.

Coral (below)
Although varying greatly in shape and size, all corals are essentially the same in composition. The corals are simply built by different species of polyp.

Coral mechanism (below)
Inside the surface of a living coral there are many individual animals called polyps.

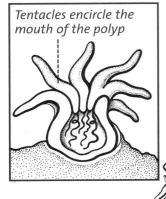

Tentacles encircle the mouth of the polyp

Single-celled animal-like organisms are known as protozoans ("first animals"). Most are microscopic, but some are visible to the naked eye.

PROTOZOANS MAY BE DESCRIBED AS free-living, parasitic (feeding from other living organisms), or symbiotic (living alongside other organisms for mutual benefit). The most familiar protozoans are called amebas. *Amoeba proteus* lives in water and is a typical form. It has a flexible cell wall, which allows it to wrap itself around items of food and take them into its body. Once inside, small stomachlike objects, called food vacuoles, digest the food. The amebas can move with the aid of limblike projections, but otherwise rely on currents in the water. Other free-living protozoans have true appendages for swimming. Some have flexible, whiplike tails called flagella, which they wiggle. Others have rows of stiff bristles called cilia, which they beat like tiny oars. One

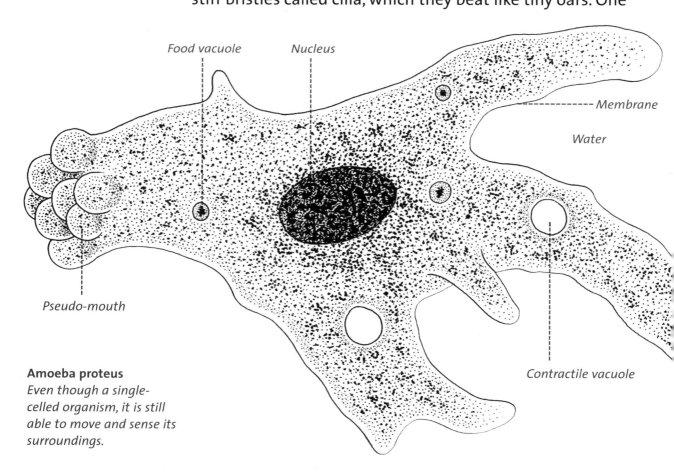

Food vacuole   Nucleus

Membrane

Water

Pseudo-mouth

Contractile vacuole

Amoeba proteus
Even though a single-celled organism, it is still able to move and sense its surroundings.

type of ameba—*Entamoeba histolytica*—causes severe diarrhea, called amebic dysentery or amebiasis. It lives in the intestinal fluid of mammals, including humans. Although this ameba is a parasitic type, there are other protozoans that actually invade the cells of plants and animals. Well-known examples are the *Plasmodium* protozoans, which cause the disease malaria. These protozoans invade cells of the liver and red blood cells, causing eventual death in the host organism.

IT'S A FACT

The malaria parasite, *Plasmodium*, has a complex life history, involving mammals and *Anopheles* mosquitoes. The parasites breed inside the mosquitoes and enter their saliva glands. The mosquitoes then introduce the parasites into the circulation of mammals when they feed on their blood. Once inside mammals, the parasites infect the liver and blood, causing malaria.

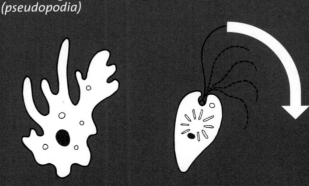

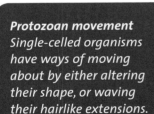

Protozoan movement
Single-celled organisms have ways of moving about by either altering their shape, or waving their hairlike extensions.

1 *Extending themselves (pseudopodia)*

2 *Whipping action*

3 *Rhythmical movement*

© DIAGRAM

The protozoans were probably succeeded by the parazoans—the first true animals. Parazoans include the poriferans or sponges. Parazoan means "beside animal" since each grows in an irregular shape or amorphous mass.

PARAZOANS ARE MULTICELLED ANIMALS (metazoans) but lack distinctly different body parts. Instead, the whole body is an even mix of cells. Nevertheless, being multicelled means that poriferans can grow far larger than single-celled animals, and they have the potential to evolve into eumetazoans ("true changed animals").

Eumetazoans, with differentiated cells, include all other animals, from corals to vertebrates.

Clearly the principle underlying eumetazoans is a highly successful formula. The reason for this success is that eumetazoans have the potential to produce an infinite variety of designs, because they have cells that are used for different purposes. Furthermore, the fact that there are living examples of most stages in eumetazoan evolution means that the potential has not been lost over time. With so many different species—an estimated 8 million—the eumetazoans can ensure that their group will survive in one way or another, given any environmental changes. In fact, they have already succeeded in surviving a number of natural disasters through prehistory as well as coping with the gradual changes of the Earth's surface—in the oceans, on the land, and in the air.

The eumetazoans are traditionally divided into 21 groups of animals, called phyla. In turn, those phyla are divided into about 80 smaller groups called classes. There is such a wide variety in form within the eumetazoan group that it would be futile to attempt to describe a typical form. The eumetazoans include corals, worms, mollusks, crabs, spiders, insects, fish, amphibians, reptiles, birds, and mammals.

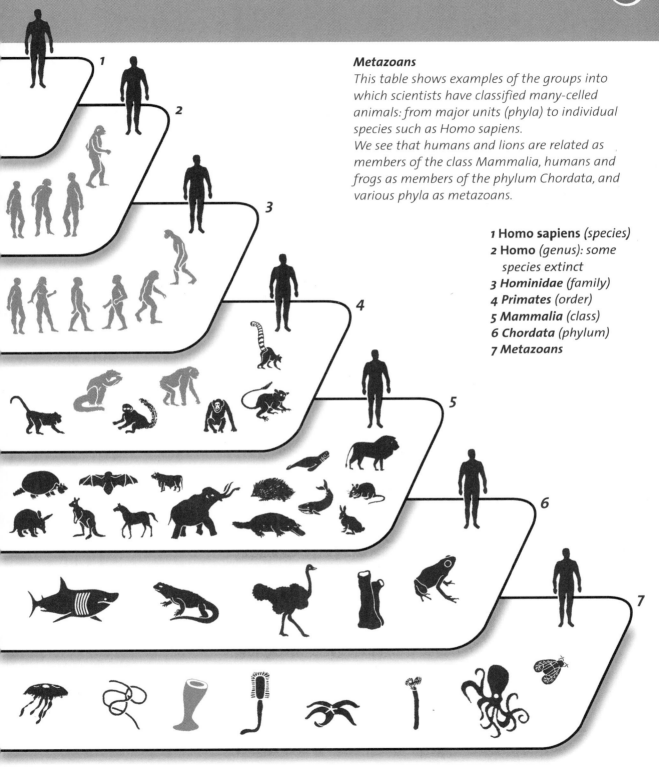

Metazoans

This table shows examples of the groups into which scientists have classified many-celled animals: from major units (phyla) to individual species such as Homo sapiens.

We see that humans and lions are related as members of the class Mammalia, humans and frogs as members of the phylum Chordata, and various phyla as metazoans.

1 **Homo sapiens** (species)
2 **Homo** (genus): some species extinct
3 **Hominidae** (family)
4 **Primates** (order)
5 **Mammalia** (class)
6 **Chordata** (phylum)
7 **Metazoans**

From soft bodies to exoskeletons

When primitive animals began to grow larger, most evolved rigid frameworks, or skeletons, to keep their shape. In fact it was protozoans that first began making skeletons, mainly as protection from other organisms intent on eating them. They use minerals to create tiny rods, called spicules, and snail-like shells.

THE PORIFERANS OR SPONGES use a rubbery material called collagen to create flexible skeletons. Coral polyps do not have skeletons but make an outer casing of mineral deposits instead. This tradition was continued in the form of snail shells. Similarly, various kinds of cephalopod feature mineral shells. The nautilus is a living example, but the fossil record includes hundreds of different ammonites and belemnites. Cuttlefish are interesting members of the group because their shells have been modified into bonelike structures. The echinoderms—starfish and sea urchins—have bonelike plates made of calcium carbonate that develop in their skin, which are either fused together or remain detached.

Soft-bodied animals (left and below)
The majority of these animals live in water, which supports the structure of their bodies.

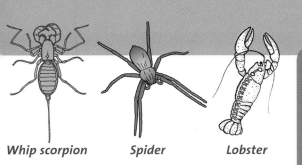

Whip scorpion   **Spider**   **Lobster**

Animals with exoskeletons (above)
Arthropod means "jointed leg" as these creatures have joints in their exoskeletons to let them move with ease.

IT'S A FACT
When an arthropod is ready to grow it needs to shed its old exoskeleton. By increasing the pressure inside, the creature splits the old exoskeleton open so that it can squeeze out. It already has its new exoskeleton, but the chitin is soft so that it can be inflated to the right size. The animal then has to wait somewhere safe from predators until the new exoskeleton has had time to harden.

Praying mantis

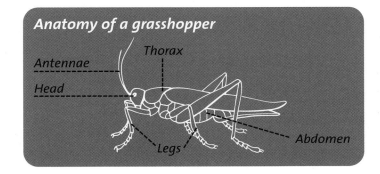

Anatomy of a grasshopper

Antennae — Head — Thorax — Legs — Abdomen

The external skeleton or "exoskeleton" really came into its own with the evolution of the arthropods. The arthropods include crabs, lobsters, insects, spiders, scorpions, millipedes, and centipedes. They all have exoskeletons made from a substance called chitin, a complex organic material. Chitin is hard, but it is tough rather than brittle, so that arthropods can cope with violent blows without the exoskeleton cracking. They have solved the problem of moving by having their exoskeletons jointed so that each part can move separately. They have also gotten around the problem of growing by discarding their old exoskeletons, and replacing them with larger ones.

© DIAGRAM

From exo-
to endoskeletons

Although many animals have exoskeletons (external skeletons), higher life-forms evolved another way of supporting their bodies: endoskeletons (internal skeletons).

EXOSKELETONS HAVE THEIR LIMITATIONS—the most obvious is ease of growth. To grow larger, animals with exoskeletons need to shed their old skeleton so that a larger one can take its place. This process leaves them vulnerable to attack because a new exoskeleton remains soft for some time. The animals are also unable to move very well during this time because their muscles need a rigid skeleton to work.

There is another problem: animals with exoskeletons can grow only to a certain size before the laws of physics prevent them from being able to move. This is because the

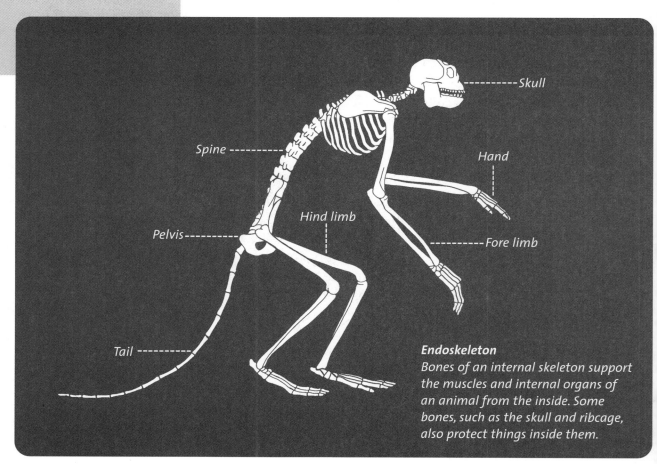

Skull

Spine

Hand

Hind limb

Pelvis

Fore limb

Tail

Endoskeleton
Bones of an internal skeleton support the muscles and internal organs of an animal from the inside. Some bones, such as the skull and ribcage, also protect things inside them.

exoskeleton needs to remain strong as it grows, and would eventually become too heavy for internal muscles to have any effect.

Endoskeletons (internal skeletons) largely solved these problems. However, the animals possessing them did not evolve from those with true exoskeletons—the arthropods. The echinoderms—starfish and sea urchins—were the first animals to have endoskeletons. They have plates of bonelike calcium carbonate embedded in their skin. So it was a fairly simple evolutionary step from echinoderms to chordates with proper endoskeletons made from cartilage or bone.

Bones are made of calcium carbonate and collagen, which is the structural protein of animal cells. The calcium carbonate makes bones hard, but also brittle. Collagen gives bones flexibility, but is soft. The combination of the two results in the toughness that bones need to cope with the stresses and strains that arise from supporting and moving an animal.

Joint

Honeycombing

Marrow cavity

Solid bone

Shaft

Bone structure
These structural features are common to every bone.

IT'S A FACT
Calcium carbonate and collagen make a material ideally suited for bones, but the material can be heavy. So bones have been adapted to use as little material as possible, without losing their strength. This is achieved by bones being hollow with supporting struts and braces to provide mechanical strength. In addition, bones often have a honeycomblike arrangement of tiny cavities to reduce weight still further.

© DIAGRAM

From invertebrates to vertebrates

The most advanced animals with no protection for their brains or nervous systems are the cephalopods: squid, cuttlefish, and octopuses. They rely on their supple bodies and intelligence to avoid injury.

THE ARTHROPODS—insects, spiders, crabs, and lobsters—possess tough exoskeletons, which provide armorlike protection for their nervous systems. In a separate line of evolution, some eumetazoans evolved an internal skeleton (endoskeleton). They had a strengthening spine of cartilage (the notochord). Above the notochord was a tubular nerve cord. Among these "chordates," some developed a skull (cranium) that protected the brain. In others, the notochord in the adult was also replaced by a series of bones—the vertebrae. Among vertebrates, some maintained a spine made of cartilage. Others evolved vertebrae made of bone. Today, lower chordates still exist as sea squirts and lancelets, while the higher chordates are fish, amphibians, reptiles, birds, and mammals.

Adapting to circumstances
There is no set plan for the layout of the nervous systems in invertebrates.

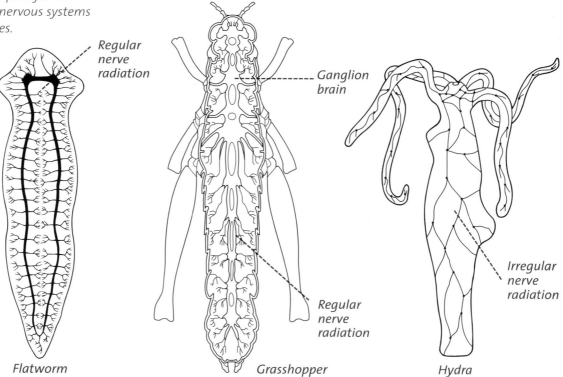

Regular nerve radiation

Ganglion brain

Regular nerve radiation

Irregular nerve radiation

Flatworm

Grasshopper

Hydra

Although the vertebrae and the skull are part of the endoskeleton in vertebrates, they also function as an exoskeleton for the spinal cord and brain, so they have a double function. As a part of the endoskeleton the vertebrae provide a central column of bones to which the rest of the skeleton is attached. As an exoskeleton they carry and protect the spinal cord so that each part of the body is supplied with its own set of nerves. Similarly, the skull provides a framework for holding the most vital sense organs (eyes, ears, nose, and tongue) while also functioning as a protective casing for the brain.

Being so complex, vertebrates with brain or spinal injuries lose their survival edge, which is why the roles of the vertebrae and skull are so important. Injury to the nervous system or skeleton is life-threatening to invertebrates too, but they have the capacity to reproduce in far greater numbers as a means of ensuring survival of their species.

IT'S A FACT
Cephalopods and arthropods are invertebrates. They have brains and nervous systems, but they are not protected by vertebrae and a skull. Fish, amphibians, birds, and mammals are vertebrates. They have spinal cords and brains hidden inside vertebrae and skull bones for their protection.

Octopus

----- *Brain*

--- *Spinal cord*

---------- *Nerves*

Following a pattern
The design of the nervous systems of vertebrates follows a set pattern.

© DIAGRAM

Fungi are neither plants nor animals. Some are single-celled. Others have bodies with various structures, but the component cells do not have discrete cell walls. Like plants, most are immobile.

AS FUNGI CANNOT PRODUCE their own food, they rely on ready-made sources of nutrition. These sources are organic substances from dead or living organisms. Most fungi feed on decaying organic matter, and play an important role in breaking down plant and animal matter (decomposition), so that components can be recycled by the environment. They are described as saprophytic fungi. Those that feed on living organisms are known as parasitic fungi. Some cause no particular harm to the host organism, but others cause disease or even death to their host. A few fungi also live in partnership with algae and are known as lichens.

The main part of a fungus plant is called the mycelium. It is made of a network of threadlike structures called hyphae. The hyphae penetrate the food source of the fungus to absorb nutrition. The mycelium of a fungus does not grow to form a particular shape, because it tends to send out hyphae in the direction of the best food supply. When fungi are ready to reproduce they develop fruiting bodies that contain spores—tiny seedlike structures. It is these fruiting bodies that distinguish one type of fungus from another.

The simplest fungi are the phycomycetes (algalike fungi). Among them are the pin molds, which produce pinlike spore-bearing bodies. The ascomycetes (sac-fungi) are slightly more

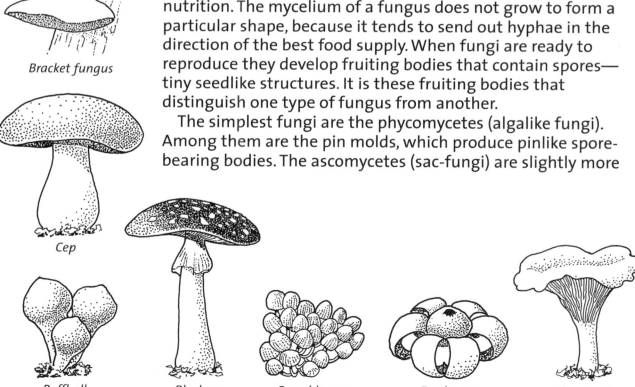

Bracket fungus

Cep

Puffball

Blusher

Crumble cap

Earth star

Chanterelle

Fly agaric
This is one of the advanced fungi,
popularly known as a toadstool. It is a
typical example of its group, and
poisonous.

advanced. They include mildews,
yeasts, morels, and truffles. These
fungi typically produce saclike,
rubbery fruits.

Finally come the advanced fungi—
basidiomycetes (basidium fungi).
They bear fruits containing clublike
structures called basidia. The
advanced fungi include toadstools,
mushrooms, puffballs, and bracket
fungi.

IT'S A FACT
Many advanced fungi have
symbiotic relationships with
trees, where both benefit
from the arrangement. The
fungi grow special "roots"
called mycorrhizae which
wrap around the tree roots.
The fungi take food from the
trees, but the trees find it
easier to absorb nutrients
from the soil.

Amethyst
deceiver

Honey fungus

Some organisms have evolved intimate relationships with others so that they work in partnership, or as composite organisms. They actually function as a single organism and cannot survive easily without each other. These relationships are described as symbiotic and work on the basis that each type of organism benefits from the arrangement. Each organism involved is known as a symbiont. Examples of these composite organisms include plant-plant, animal-animal, and animal-plant combinations.

THE MOST FAMILIAR COMPOSITE organisms are the lichens, which are partly fungus, partly alga. Each type of organism plays a particular role in the partnership. The alga is capable of photosynthesis, because it contains chlorophyll, so it provides food for both. In return, the fungus provides protection for the alga, because it can conserve moisture and block harmful rays from the Sun.

In the animal kingdom the Portuguese man-of-war is a good example of a composite organism. Each part of its body is made from the cells of a different kind of polyp. By working together the polyps manage to move about, catch prey, and digest it as food. The different polyps are so intimately involved that the composite organism even has its own scientific name—*Physalis physalis*.

Examples of animal-alga composite organisms are certain kinds of sponges and hydras. Although the animal organisms are dominant in the

IT'S A FACT
By joining forces to create lichens, fungi and algae manage to live in places where other organisms cannot survive. For example, lichens can be found on the surfaces of rocks and buildings where nutrients are very scarce.

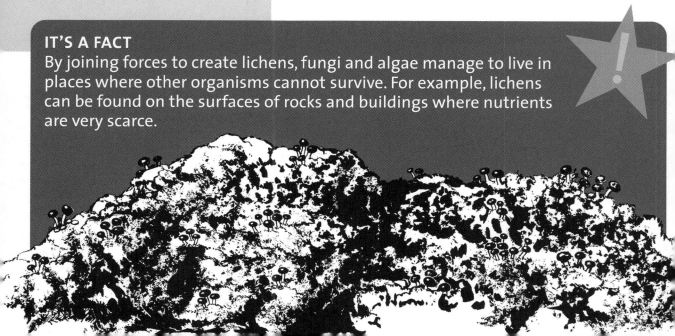

relationship, some species of sponge and hydra contain algae, just like the lichens, and for the same reason. In return for the food that the algae provide, the animals provide the algae with protection from being eaten by aquatic herbivores, such as snails.

In addition, there are animals that harbor microorganisms in their digestive tracts, from which they benefit. Many herbivorous mammals are known to have symbiotic relationships with such microorganisms. The microorganisms break down the cellulose of greenery, which the herbivores eat, into digestible compounds upon which both organisms can then feed.

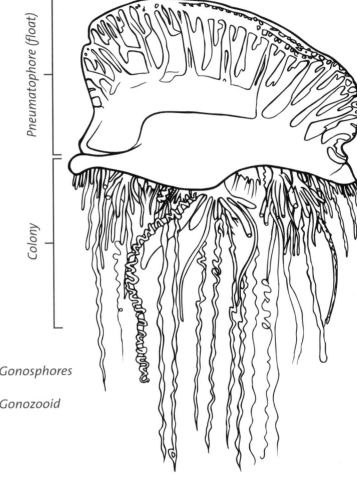

Pneumatophore (float)

Colony

Portuguese man-of-war
Despite appearances, this "organism" is actually a colony of different organisms working together to survive.

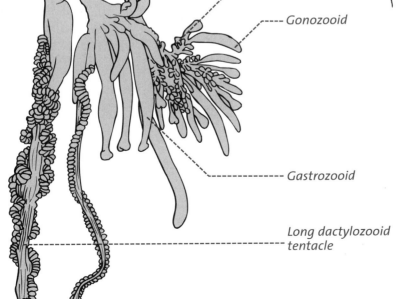

Gonosphores

Gonozooid

Gastrozooid

Long dactylozooid tentacle

© DIAGRAM

The simplest organisms capable of photosynthesis come as single-celled and multicelled algae. Algae have three groups—green algae, brown algae, and red algae. All three occur as seaweeds.

GREEN ALGAE INCLUDE the lowliest true plants. Next on the evolutionary ladder come the bryophytes, otherwise known as mosses and liverworts. Unlike algae, they live on land, although most species still require moist habitats. The bryophytes lack proper roots, and grip surfaces with rootlike threads called rhizoids. They are typically low-growing, creating mats or carpets of greenery over appropriate surfaces. Both liverworts and mosses produce spores instead of seeds.

Mosses are slightly more advanced than liverworts, as they have stems and leaves. This indicates that they gave rise to the next group of plants, the pteridophytes, which include ferns, brackens, horsetails, tree ferns, clubmosses, quillworts, and psilotes. The pteridophytes were the group

IT'S A FACT
Simple plants produce spores rather than seeds. Spores contain the genetic information to grow new plants just like seeds, but they lack a food supply. Although disadvantageous to a plant when it begins to grow, as an adult it can use up fewer resources in reproduction, by production of spores.

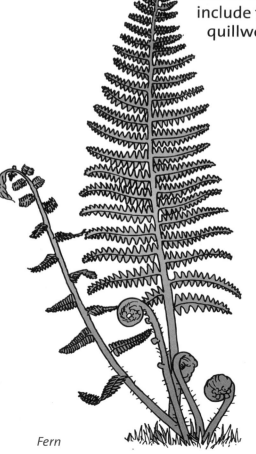

Fern

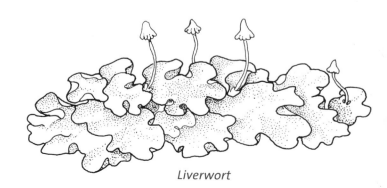

Liverwort

of plants that first colonized actual dry land. Like mosses, the adult plants still produce spores instead of seeds, but they evolved a vitally important characteristic that made them so much more successful. This was the presence of water-conducting cells in their stems and leaves. It meant that they could live in dry places, and grow to the size of trees, yet still transport water from the ground to their farthest extremities.

As well as by spore production, many pteridophytes reproduce by sending out special roots called rhizomes. They spread from the parent plants, raising new shoots here and there, so that the area is colonized. In swampy places, where rhizomes and spores are not an effective means of reproduction, some species produce small plantlets from their leaves or fronds. These drop into the water and drift about until they manage to take root some distance away.

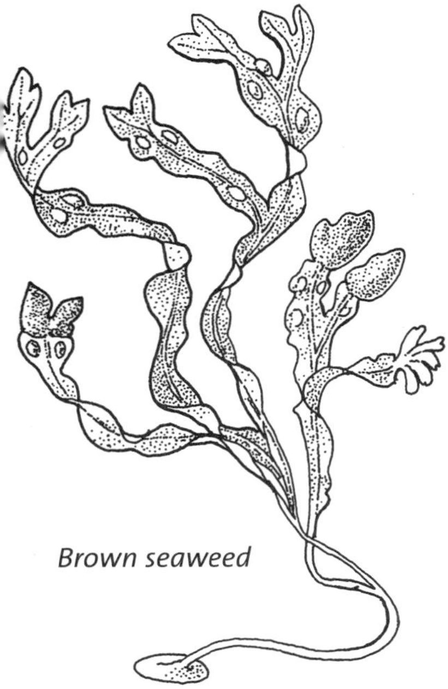

Brown seaweed

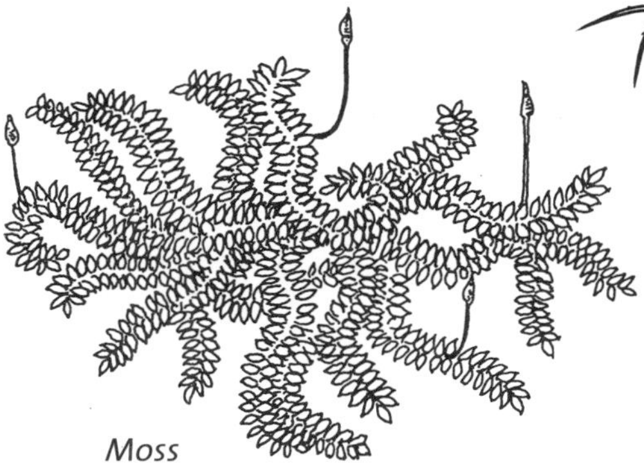

Moss

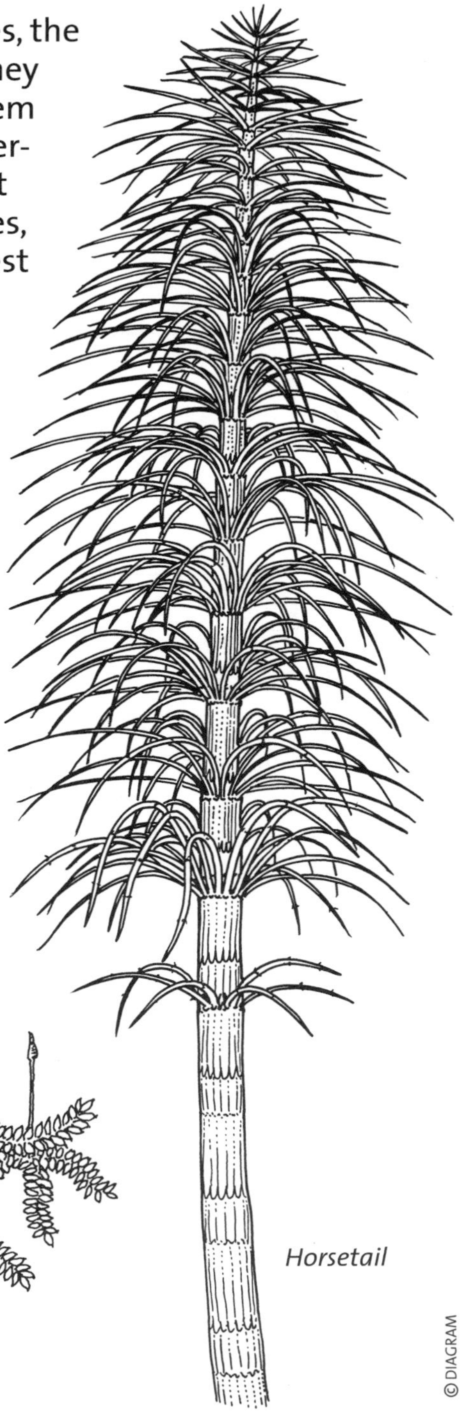

Horsetail

© DIAGRAM

The first seed-producing plants are known as gymnosperms ("naked seeds"). They derive their name from having seeds that lack a husk or shell. Instead the seeds are typically protected by a woody fruit, called a cone, until they are ready to germinate. Others produce berrylike fruits that surround their seeds.

AMONG THE GYMNOSPERMS are the firs, pines, cedars, larches, sequoias, spruces, cypresses, cycads, hemlocks, junipers, yews, monkey-puzzle, and maidenhair or ginkgo.

Cycads are the most primitive of the gymnosperms, looking very similar to tree ferns. The trunk grows in such a way that old leaves fall to leave rings of scars as the trees becomes taller. The conifers are the largest gymnosperm group. Fir trees, such as those used for Christmas trees, are a typical example: they are evergreen and have needle-like leaves. These are adaptations for survival on dry or frozen soils, where deciduous trees find it hard to live because of the lack of a sufficient water supply, and a short growing season. Most conifers grow in the Northern Hemisphere, especially around

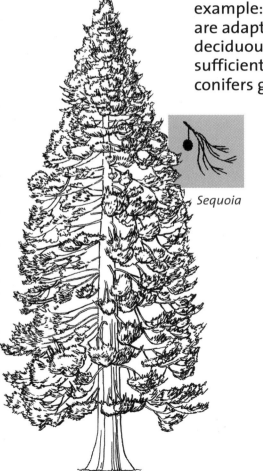

Sequoia

Cypress

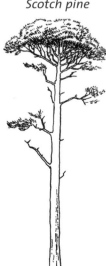

Scotch pine

Larch

the Arctic Circle and the Mediterranean Sea. A few conifers are found in the Southern Hemisphere, though. A well known example is the *Araucaria* or monkey-puzzle tree of the Andes mountains. It derived its common name because of its unique leaves. They are sharply pointed and arranged in rings so that a monkey would find the tree difficult to climb.

The maidenhair or ginkgo tree, from China, is a gymnosperm that looks very much like a fruit tree from a distance. Up close, though, it has unusual leaves which are arranged into a fan-like shape. It is known as the duck's foot tree in China for this reason.

A group of gymnosperms called gnetales seem to represent the intermediate evolutionary step to flowering plants. They have leaves like those of flowering plants, but they still produce seed cones.

IT'S A FACT
Junipers and yews have evolved a technique for dispersing their seeds, which is far more common in flowering plants and trees. They surround their seeds with a fleshy substance to attract hungry birds. The birds swallow the seeds whole, then excrete them some distance away from the parent tree, ready for germination.

Douglas fir   *Ginkgo*

Yew

The most advanced group of plants are commonly known as the flowering plants.

THIS DESCRIPTION, although true, is not exclusive to the group, as many gymnosperm plants also have flowers. However, the scientific name for the flowering plants—angiosperms—is more appropriate. It means "contained seeds," because their seeds always include a protective shell or husk—the testa. Angiosperm seeds vary in size from tiny specks to that of the coconut. Their size is not related to the scale of the plant, but has to do with the plant's method of dissemination (dispersal or spreading of seeds) and how much investment of nutrition a parent plant puts into each seed. There is a trade-off, because larger seeds are produced in fewer numbers, and travel less easily, but they stand a better chance of establishing themselves as new plants.

Seeds are packaged in numerous ways to aid dissemination. Many are enclosed inside a fruit of one description or another. The flesh of the fruit is designed to be an attractive food for animals. When animals take the fruit they carry the seeds away from the parent plant. Seeds may then be discarded onto the ground, or they may even travel through the animals' digestive systems before finding somewhere to grow. Seeds described as nuts use a similar strategy.

Banana
This palmlike plant is a primitive angiosperm, or flowering plant.

Pomegranate
Shown in cross-section, this is a typical angiosperm fruit. The encased seeds can be clearly seen within.

Some are eaten and destroyed by animals, but others are buried and forgotten so that they are planted and ready to grow. Other seeds are carried away by wind, or stick temporarily to the fur of passing creatures.

Angiosperms are divided into two broad groups, according to their seed structures. They are the monocotyledons ("one cotyledon") and dicotyledons ("two cotyledons"). A cotyledon is the part of a seed embryo which emerges as a temporary leaf (seed leaf) when it germinates and begins to grow.

IT'S A FACT
The monocotyledons are less advanced and include grasses, lilies, and palms. The dicotyledons are a far larger group. Included are all broad-leaved trees and shrubs, plus many families of flowers such as the cabbage, buttercup, pink, dock, carrot, primrose, and daisy families, to name but a few.

Grasses
These are familiar examples of the monocotyledon group of plants.

Primrose
Garden flowers are usually members of the dicotyledon group of plants.

© DIAGRAM

Grouping plants and animals

THE FIRST SCIENTIST to attempt this was a Swedish botanist called Carolus Linnaeus. In 1753 he invented a system of grouping species according to their visual similarities. He introduced the now familiar scientific Latin double names (for genus and species), such as that of humans—*Homo sapiens* ("wise human"). In 1789 a French botanist, Antoine Jussieu, improved on the system by comparing the internal structures of species as well as their outward appearance. In 1813 a Swiss botanist, Augustin de Candolle named the system "taxonomic classification."

Since then, the system has undergone a few adjustments as scientists have made new discoveries. One such discovery was that species can have similar characteristics by coincidence and not because they are related. This is called convergent evolution. On the other hand, related species can appear to be very different in their adult form, but show their similarities during development. This is known as recapitulation. For example, larvae of crustaceans look very similar, but the adults may be as different as crabs and barnacles. So it became clear that the taxonomic classification of species might not necessarily be accurate, because it relied on scientists' points of view. This problem gave rise to the modern form of taxonomic classification known as cladistics.

Cladistics works by focusing on evolutionary relatedness in species, as is shown by fossil evidence and molecular studies of living organisms. It compares all anatomical features, and groups organisms into "clades" on

Antelope and kangaroo
In both taxonomy and cladistics, these two herbivores are classed as mammals. While the antelope is a placental mammal and the kangaroo a marsupial, they share a hypothetical common ancestor.

IT'S A FACT

Convergent evolution is where unrelated species happen to evolve with similar characteristics because they live in similar habitats, but in different places. The marsupials, or pouched mammals of Australasia, include many species that have evolved in similar ways to placental mammals on other continents.

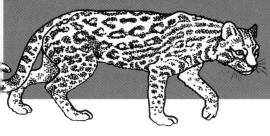

Ocelot and quoll
While one is a placental mammal and the other a marsupial mammal, both evolved to hunt small animals in forest habitats.

the basis of similar sets of inherited features. The rules were first outlined in 1950 by the German entomologist, Willi Hennig. Cladistics has been adopted by modern science as it shows more precisely than the hierarchical rankings of class, order, family, and so on, how one group of organisms is related to another. It uses branching diagrams called cladograms. The system is made workable by some compromise between the traditional and new approaches.

Anteater and numbat
Although both of these animals have specialized in feeding on ants and termites, they are unrelated and live on different continents.

© DIAGRAM

The system of taxonomic classification uses a layered structure of groups, which divide repeatedly to form a chart, which is often called a "life tree".

A LIFE TREE HAS a "trunk," "branches," and "twigs." The result is that each type of animal or plant belongs to its own series of groups from one end of the tree to the other. It is possible, therefore, to understand the relationships between species in a visual way.

The largest such groups are kingdoms—the animal kingdom and the plant kingdom for example (although both belong to the Eukaryotes, which with Archaea and Bacteria, are often regarded as super-groups known as domains). Traditional groupings continue from phylum, class, family, genus, down to species. In the case of a human, the sequence is kingdom: Animalia; phylum: Chordata; class: Mammalia; family: Hominidae; genus: *Homo*; species: *Homo sapiens*.

Traditional taxonomy looks for visual similarities between fossil and living species to establish evolutionary relationships. Cladistics exhaustively compares all anatomical features and uses fossil and molecular evidence to find likely shared ancestors. Cladistics is now generally accepted to be scientifically more accurate, but it does give some unexpected results. For example, living terrestrial vertebrates are not divided into Amphibia, Reptilia, Aves (birds), and Mammalia, but into Amphibia, Mammalia, Testudines (turtles), Lepidosauria (lizards, snakes, tuataras), Crocodylia (crocodiles, alligators, and gavials), and Aves. So birds and crocodiles are both, cladistically, reptiles. This also makes birds descendants of dinosaurs.

Cayman
Members of the crocodile family are reptiles related to birds.

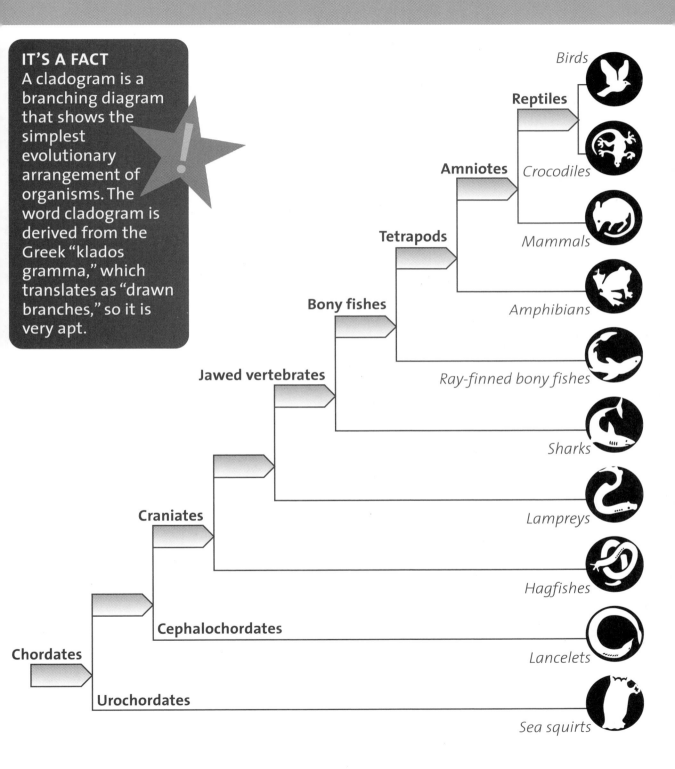

IT'S A FACT
A cladogram is a branching diagram that shows the simplest evolutionary arrangement of organisms. The word cladogram is derived from the Greek "klados gramma," which translates as "drawn branches," so it is very apt.

Birds

Reptiles

Amniotes

Crocodiles

Tetrapods

Mammals

Bony fishes

Amphibians

Jawed vertebrates

Ray-finned bony fishes

Sharks

Craniates

Lampreys

Hagfishes

Cephalochordates

Lancelets

Chordates

Urochordates

Sea squirts

When biologists use the term "evolution," they are referring to the process by which the design of organisms changes over hundreds, thousands, or millions of years—they evolve.

EVOLUTION HAPPENS BY CHANCE but it ensures survival of life in the face of ongoing changes to the environment. The word itself was coined in 1852 by the British natural philosopher, Herbert Spencer. He derived it from the Latin *evolvere* which means "to roll out."

During the 1700s, some people realized that animals and plants had an ability to evolve, because fossils differed from living species. In 1809 the French biologist, Jean-Baptiste de Lamarck, came up with the first theory to explain evolution. He thought that animals could acquire new characteristics during their own lifetimes and pass them on to their offspring—just like an athlete developing a muscular body by training and then producing naturally-muscular children. It was an idea that seemed logical on the surface, but it actually had no scientific basis. So, Lamarckism—as his theory became known—was

Natural selection in action
Creatures that avoid dying before reproduction are the ones selected by nature to pass on their genes.

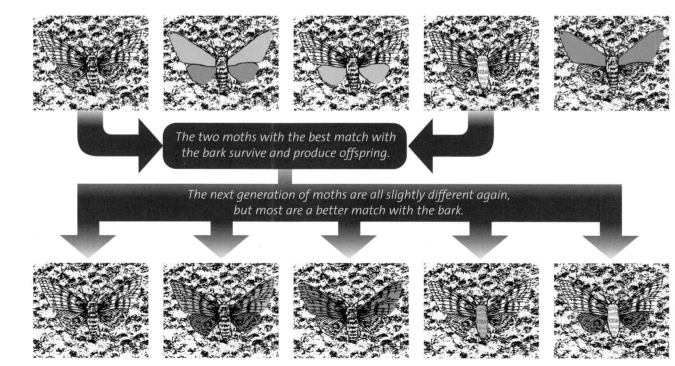

The two moths with the best match with the bark survive and produce offspring.

The next generation of moths are all slightly different again, but most are a better match with the bark.

Apapana

Liwi

BACK IN TIME
Since Darwin's time, evolutionary theory has been influenced by scientific progress. On the one hand, much more is known about the mechanism behind evolution—genetics. On the other hand, certain new ideas have emerged that modify the theory. For example, there is the idea of punctuated equilibrium, which suggests that evolution occurs in fits and starts—saltation.

Akiapolauu

Honeycreepers
The variety seen in the bills of the honeycreepers' species is a good example of divergent evolution. They have each adapted from an ancestral form to exploit available food sources.

Ancestral honeycreeper

Ou

ultimately dismissed when the British naturalist, Charles Darwin, published his own theory in 1859.

Darwinism differs from Lamarckism by stating that new characteristics are inherited from parents and not acquired during a lifetime. Darwin suggested that animals and plants from the same species all vary very slightly and that this was the secret to evolution. Nature favors those individuals inheriting the features best suited to an environment with the consequence that a species evolves very gradually over time by "survival of the fittest." He published his theory as *The Origin of Species by Natural Selection*. All the scientific evidence gathered since then has shown that Darwin was correct. Darwin is therefore described as the "father of evolutionary theory" in honor of his genius.

Grosbeak finch

Kauai akioloa

Maui parrotbill

Although evolutionary theory is frequently referred to as Darwinism, after the British naturalist, Charles Darwin (1809–82), the fundamental principle of natural selection was independently realized by another British naturalist and contemporary of Darwin—Alfred Russel Wallace (1823–1913).

Alfred Russel Wallace

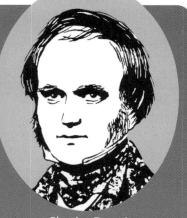

Charles Darwin

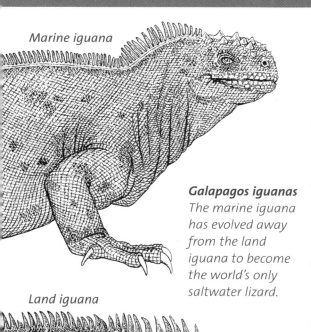

Marine iguana

Land iguana

Galapagos iguanas
The marine iguana has evolved away from the land iguana to become the world's only saltwater lizard.

DARWIN was a self-taught naturalist from a wealthy background. In 1831–34 he circumnavigated the world as ship's naturalist aboard *HMS Beagle*. During the voyage the idea of natural selection occurred to him, and he began gathering scientific evidence to back up his theory. He was particularly inspired by a visit to the Galapagos Islands, situated west of equatorial South America. He saw that each island had its own types of tortoise and finch, and it seemed likely that each had evolved from one original tortoise and finch species. When he returned to England, he continued his painstaking search for evidence, using domestic types of dove to show that artificial selection causes evolution in the same way.

Wallace was also a self-taught naturalist, but from a less privileged family. He became interested in natural history, having forged a living by selling exotic animals to English collectors and zoos. While on an expedition in Southeast Asia he also hit on the idea of natural selection. He was so excited by his idea that he actually wrote to Darwin in 1858 to see whether the idea had any real credibility in scientific terms.

When Darwin received Wallace's letter he had spent twenty-five years working on his theory, but had not yet published it. In an age of religious doctrine, he had wanted to be absolutely sure of his facts to defend himself against the barrage of objection and ridicule he knew he would receive from the polite society to which he belonged. Wallace's letter shocked Darwin into action however, and he published *The Origin of Species by Natural Selection* in 1859.

BACK IN TIME
Darwin almost became a clergyman before joining *HMS Beagle*. He realized the full implications of his theory, and understood the charge of blasphemy which was placed at his door. He suffered from anxiety-related illness for the remainder of his life.

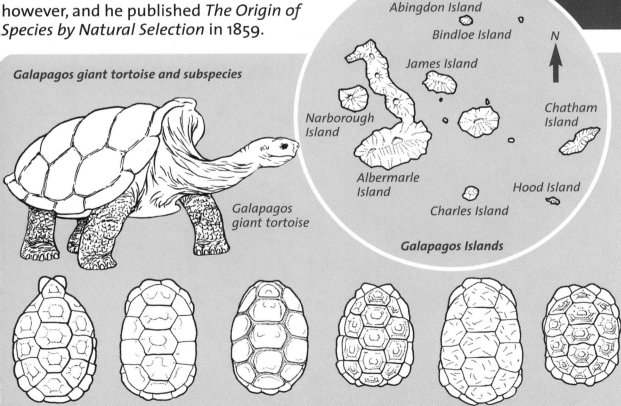

Galapagos giant tortoise and subspecies

Galapagos giant tortoise

Abingdon Island
Bindloe Island
James Island
N
Narborough Island
Chatham Island
Albermarle Island
Hood Island
Charles Island

Galapagos Islands

Abingdon Island

Albermarle Island

Charles Island

Hood Island

Chatham Island

James Island

© DIAGRAM

The first scientist to begin unraveling the mystery of genetics was the Austrian Gregor Mendel (1822–84). He conducted experiments with pea plants that demonstrated the inheritance of characteristics from one generation by the next in a mathematically predictable way.

THE AUSTRIAN SCIENTIST Gregor Mendel concluded that there must be invisible packages of information being passed from the parent plants to their offspring, which he called particles. Mendel published his work in 1865, but remained virtually unknown until his work was rediscovered in 1900 by two botanists. By then microscopy had begun to reveal the structure of nuclei. The word chromosome was coined in 1888, and in 1909 a Dutch botanist, Wilhelm Johannsen (1857–1927), described Mendel's "particles" as "genes" for the first time, so genetics was born. "Gene" derives from the Greek word *genos*, meaning "offspring."

The following year—1910—saw a U.S. geneticist, Thomas Hunt Morgan (1866–1945), demonstrate the role of chromosomes in inheritance. By 1950 the gene-building molecule had been identified and named DNA (deoxyribonucleic acid), but its physical structure was not known.

Human chromosomes
The molecules that store the code for making animals or plants—DNA—are so long that they need to be tied up into bundles, called chromosomes. They then take up less space in the nucleus, and also avoid becoming tangled up with each other.

The breakthrough came in 1953. British biophysicist Francis Crick (1916–), and U.S. biologist James Watson (1928–), were able to propose a model for the DNA structure. The model was based on X-ray crystallographs of DNA, taken by British scientists Rosalind Franklin (1920–58) and Maurice Wilkins (1916–).

The DNA model resembles a ladder twisted to form a double helix. Each rung of the ladder is made from a pair of molecules in one of four combinations: adenine + thymine; thymine + adenine; guanine + cytosine; and cytosine + guanine. Their proportions and order are unique for each species. DNA therefore holds information in a double-binary form, so that its molecules have to be extremely long to store the amount of information required to build an organism. For this reason, each DNA strand is coiled up several times to save space, and also to help prevent damage.

IT'S A FACT
Although DNA stores all of the information for building an organism, there is another molecule which is responsible for achieving the same effect. RNA (ribonucleic acid) acts as a messenger by carrying sections of information from the DNA so that proteins can be constructed or synthesized from amino acids.

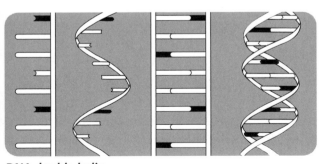

DNA double helix
Although DNA can store complex information, it has a very simple, ladderlike, structure known as the double helix.

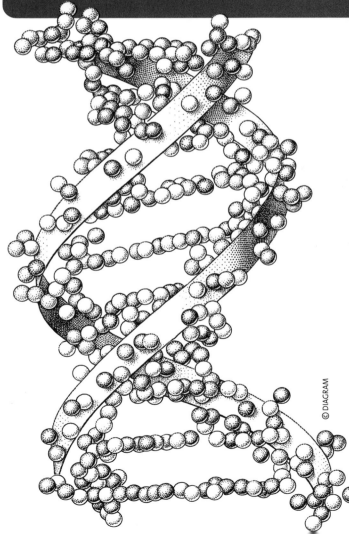

© DIAGRAM

There are about eight million living animal species, with another million plants. That may seem a lot, but the Earth has witnessed countless more millions of species come and go, because extinction is part of nature.

WITH SO MANY SPECIES of plant and animal all attempting to survive, it is inevitable that some species are out-competed by others over the course of time. Or they cannot evolve quickly enough when environments change.

It is what scientists call "reaching an evolutionary dead end." Rather than becoming no longer suitably adapted to their environment however, some species evolved sufficiently different characteristics to give rise to new species. Some of these became the ancestors of species living today. Either way, the original species became extinct.

When scientists talk of environmental changes, they are referring to a number of factors. The most obvious changes are those that can occur relatively suddenly and dramatically, such as earthquakes, volcanic eruptions, or meteor strikes. Although these natural disasters are known to have caused extinction, it is the subtle and gradual changes that have had a greater effect in the long term.

Changes in climate causing expansion and contraction of the polar regions, breakup of the continental landmasses, and changes in the Earth's magnetic field, have all had a profound effect on the survival of animal and plant species. Because all living things interact with one another, a decline in the population of one species can prompt the rise or fall of another's. The balance of nature is very delicate.

Parasaurolophus
This is just one of countless millions of species now extinct.

Present day

Flat areas represent extinctions

Bottlenecks represent the survival of ancestral species.

BACK IN TIME
Ancestral species are those that gave rise to living species. In practice they were very lucky to have done so, because it takes only a single species to give rise to new groups. For example, the dinosaurs must all have evolved from a single ancestral species, while all of its related species became extinct. The same is true of the mammals, sharing one common ancestor. Similarly, the birds have evolved from just one dinosaur species that managed to avoid extinction.

© DIAGRAM

The term "living fossil" is often used to describe contemporary species that have changed little since the time they first evolved. It is also used in describing plants and animals that are the sole surviving representatives of their kind. The fact that they still exist is a testament to how well suited they are to their habitats, or how little their particular habitats have changed since they first evolved.

IN THE ANIMAL KINGDOM the classic example is the coelacanth (*Latimeria chalumnae*). The coelacanth is related to chordates that gave rise to the evolution of land vertebrates. Coelacanths were actually thought to be entirely extinct until the first specimen was reported to science in 1938. A number of individuals have since been caught and it seems that most of them live at some depth off volcanic islands between Madagascar and Africa. Evidently such habitats have remained virtually unchanged for 380 million years, since the Devonian period, when the first known coelacanths lived.

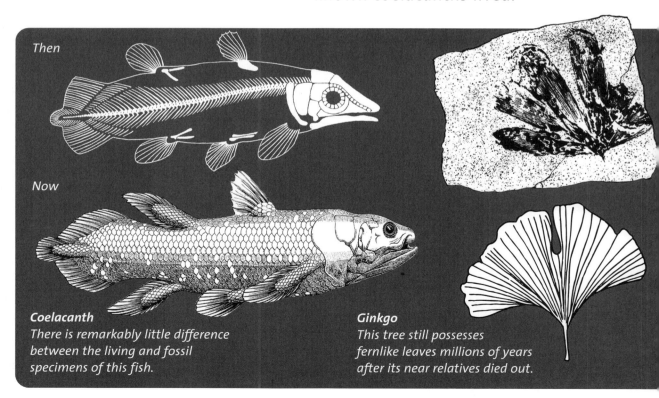

Then

Now

Coelacanth
There is remarkably little difference between the living and fossil specimens of this fish.

Ginkgo
This tree still possesses fernlike leaves millions of years after its near relatives died out.

In the plant kingdom the best known example is the maidenhair tree or ginkgo (*Ginkgo biloba*). The tree is the one surviving member of a family that is thought to mark the transition from gymnosperms to flowering trees. It originates from China, where it has managed to survive with relatively little change since the Jurassic period about 150 million years ago, the time from which fossils of similar trees emanate.

There are plenty of groups of animals and plants that have changed relatively little since their point of origin too. A great many invertebrates are similar to their fossilized counterparts. Those fossilized in amber—usually insects and spiders—are seen to be almost exact replicas of living examples, despite the intervening millions of years. Sharks and crocodiles are also extremely close to the forms of their fossil ancestors.

IT'S A FACT
Among the nonflowering plants there are plenty of fossil look-alikes, which are even used for the backdrops in films and television programs about prehistoric life. Tree ferns and cycads are particular favorites for dinosaur movies.

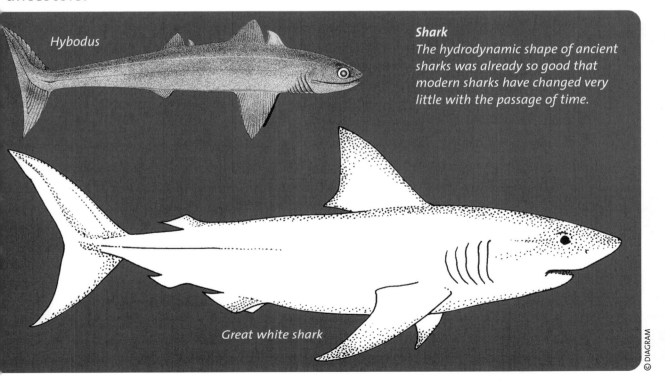

Hybodus

Shark
The hydrodynamic shape of ancient sharks was already so good that modern sharks have changed very little with the passage of time.

Great white shark

© DIAGRAM

Equipped with DNA, early organisms had the means to duplicate themselves accurately. However, when they began reproducing sexually, each parent contributed half of its DNA to its offspring. This gave rise to new generations of individuals that varied from one another very slightly.

VARIATION WAS, and still is, the basis of natural selection. So, as soon as organisms competed with each other for resources, space, mates, and so on, natural selection caused the species to evolve more advanced forms. The "natural arms race" is the way this phenomenon is often described, because different species become involved in a perpetual struggle to out-perform each other. Evolutionary change is rapid since progress in one species leads to similar progress in others, so that all species are locked in a continuous cycle of improvement.

Whether they are plants or animals, all of the species within a particular habitat are part of the character or environment of that habitat. The environmental changes that promote evolution can therefore include the way organisms themselves affect a habitat. They are known as organic agents or

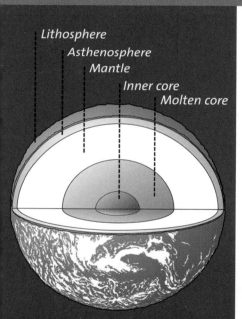

Structure of the Earth
This diagram shows that the Earth is essentially a ball of hot liquid surrounded by a solid crust. As such, the crust is constantly altering due to movement below, which is why the landmasses have shifted.

Lithosphere
Asthenosphere
Mantle
Inner core
Molten core

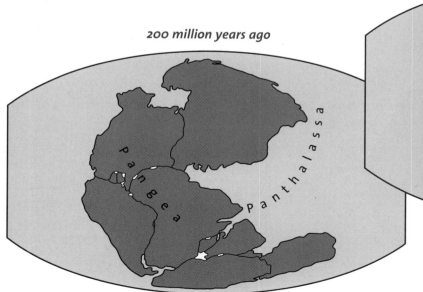

200 million years ago

Pangea

Panthalassa

rces. Other forces are inorganic. They are the esult of climatic and geological alterations. They an occur on a small or large scale, suddenly or lowly, and temporarily or permanently, depending n their nature.

An example of environmental change brought bout by organic forces is the way bacteria ransformed the Earth's primitive atmosphere into ne rich in oxygen. Millions of years later, this nade it possible for plants and animals to evolve. nvironmental change brought about by inorganic orces is typified by the geological process of plate ectonics. As landmasses moved across the surface f the Earth and split up or collided, forests ecame deserts, deserts became grasslands, and oastlines became mountain ranges.

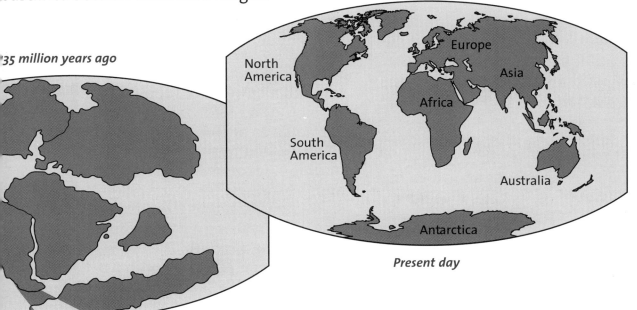

35 million years ago

Present day

The moving world
The landmasses have moved a great deal since prehistoric times, and are still on the move today.

© DIAGRAM

As one might expect, the most primitive multicelled animals are very simple in design. Although they are composed of cells that specialize in different functions, they are not specialized to a high degree. Also, they are generally soft-bodied creatures, although many are capable of creating hard structures, either internally or externally.

IT'S A FACT
Comb jellies are so called because they possess eight comblike ridges on their bodies. The comb "teeth" are cilia (hairlike structures) which vibrate so that the creatures can swim. Most comb jellies live among the zooplankton of oceans as they are very small. The largest species is the ribbonlike Venus's girdle (*Cestum veneris*), which reaches about 60 inches (150 cm) in length.

Comb jelly

SOFT-BODIED CREATURES that lack shells are often divided into three phyla: Porifera (sponges); Cnidaria (corals, sea anemones, and jellyfishes); and Ctenophora (comb jellies). Nearly all species live in marine environments, with a few having adapted to freshwater.

Sponges are not obviously animals. The Greek philosopher Aristotle was the first person to realize that they had certain animal characteristics, but his idea was dismissed until science was able to provide conclusive evidence in the 1800s. During medieval times, sponges were even thought to be lumps of solidified sea foam. Sponges range in size dramatically, and feed by filtering nutrients from the water in which they live. To do this they pump the water with millions of choanocyte chambers through a network of tubes and cavities called the aquiferous system.

Corals, sea anemones, and jellyfish are characterized by sharing life cycles that each include two forms. These are the polyp form and the medusa form. The polyp form is a stalked creature that fixes itself to a surface, and feeds by using a ring of tentacles surrounding a mouth. The medusa form is a free-swimming creature with a bell-shaped body and tubular mouth, surrounded by tentacles. Jellyfishes are familiar to us in their medusa form, while corals and sea anemones are familiar in their polyp form. The tentacles of a medusa or polyp are armed with stinging cells called cnidoblasts, which paralyze fast-moving prey.

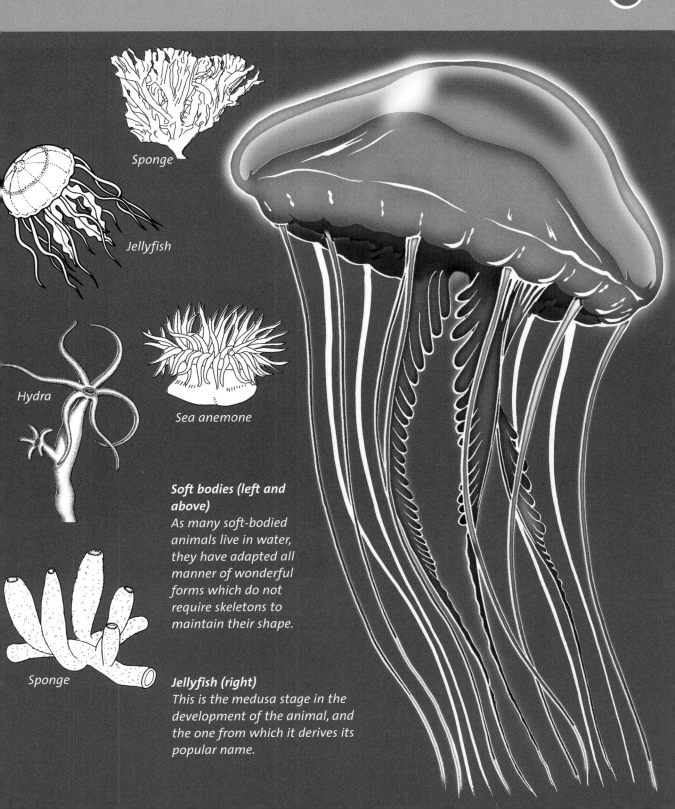

Sponge

Jellyfish

Hydra

Sea anemone

Sponge

Soft bodies (left and above)
As many soft-bodied animals live in water, they have adapted all manner of wonderful forms which do not require skeletons to maintain their shape.

Jellyfish (right)
This is the medusa stage in the development of the animal, and the one from which it derives its popular name.

Worms come in an array of different forms, but they are called worms because they all have elongated, soft bodies.

WORMS CAN BE DIVIDED conveniently into simple worms, tube worms, and complex worms. Each of these comprises a number of phyla. The simple worms are: *Platyhelminthes* (flatworms); *Nemertea* (ribbon worms); *Aschelminthes* (roundworms); and *Acanthocephala* (thorny-headed worms). The tube worms are: *Entoprocta* (entoprocts); *Bryozoa* (moss animals); and *Phoronida* (horseshoe worms). The complex worms are: *Sipuncula* (peanut worms); *Echiura* (spoon worms); and *Annelida* (segmented worms).

Flatworms are so called because they have a flat profile in cross-section. A few species are bottom-dwelling in aquatic habitats, but the majority are parasites on higher organisms. For example, *Taenia solium* is the human tapeworm. Ribbon worms are ribbonlike, and can vary dramatically in length. Most species live in marine or freshwater habitats. Roundworms are very small and live in the mud or

Tapeworm (left)
This is a parasitic worm with hooks on its head for anchoring itself inside the intestines of vertebrates.

Green ragworm

Sandworm

Common earthworm

soil of aquatic or terrestrial habitats. Some are parasitic, for example, the thorny-headed worms are adapted as gut parasites in vertebrates.

Peanut worms have rather bulbous bodies that are reminiscent of the pods in which peanuts or groundnuts grow. They burrow and feed in the mud and sand of seabeds. Spoon worms are typically sausage-shaped with a spoonlike proboscis (snout). Most live in burrows on the seabed. The Innkeeper (*Urechis caupo*) is remarkable for providing shelter and food for other organisms—another worm, a clam, a goby fish, and two types of crab. Segmented worms are the most advanced of the worms. They include the earthworms, ragworms, sea mice, and leeches. Segmented worms live in marine, freshwater, and terrestrial habitats. They use an arrangement of circular and longitudinal muscles to propel themselves in their chosen direction.

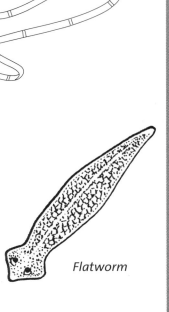
Tapeworm

Flatworm

Design for living (right and above)
The basic design of the worm has been adapted to suit a variety of different habitats and lifestyles.

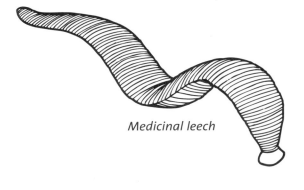
Medicinal leech

© DIAGRAM

WATER BEARS are so-named because they have rounded, bearlike bodies with four pairs of stumpy legs equipped with claws or toes. Of the 400 species none is larger than 0.05 inches (1.25 mm). They typically live in moist habitats, among plants in aquatic and terrestrial environments. Water bears have a segmented body, like annelid worms, and a chitinous exoskeleton.

There are several phyla of animals that have unusual combinations of wormlike characteristics. They include the water bears (Tardigrada), acorn worms and arrow worms (Chaetognatha), and the bearded worms (Pogonophora). Water bears are related to aquatic arthropods but appear to have worm ancestors.

Water bears
Otherwise known by the name of tardigrades, these creatures differ from worms by having limbs.

Bearded worms differ from segmented worms by having distinct parts to their bodies, rather than repeated segments. The head end is called the cephalic lobe and has many fine tentacles—the "beard." The trunk or body is attached to the head by a neck, called the bridle. At the tail end there is a section called the opisthosoma. All bearded worms inhabit marine habitats, where they live inside chitinous tubes which they make in the ocean floor. Arrow worms have lateral fins and a tail for

Bearded worm

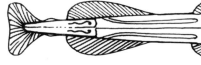

Arrow worm

swimming, making them look something like miniature arrows. Their heads are dome-shaped with rings of hooks and teeth. Arrow worms have simple eyes that enable them to hunt by sight. They feed on planktonic crustaceans. Acorn worms come in two general types. Some are distinctly wormlike and live in burrows on the sea floor. The others are similar to moss animals and coral polyps, having evolved to live inside coral-like, tubular structures. The proboscis (snout) of the wormlike forms is typically attached to the body by a narrow stalk, giving it an acornlike appearance.

Acorn worm

All mollusks are soft bodied, but they often have calcareous (calcium carbonate) shells for protection from predators.

THE PHYLUM Mollusca contains six main groups. They are: Monoplacophora (flatshells); Polyplacophora (chitons); Scaphopoda (tusk shells); Gastropoda (snails and slugs); Bivalvia (mussels and clams); and Cephalopoda (octopuses and squid).

Flatshells are regarded as living fossils. They are very similar to the fossil ancestor of the mollusk group, having a simple domed shell which is held against the surface of smooth rocks. Chitons are equipped with segmented shells, which can be rolled up as protection, in the manner of a wood louse, if the creatures are dislodged. Tusk shells are mollusks that live in tusk-shaped shells, which are buried in sandy seabeds. The open end faces downward, and a muscular foot holds the shell in position.

Snails and slugs, or gastropods, are more evolved than the previous three classes. They include limpets, top shells, winkles, cowries, whelks, sea slugs, land snails and slugs, and pond snails. In these groups the muscular foot becomes adapted for locomotion in aquatic and terrestrial habitats. In addition the senses become more highly developed, with tentacles and eyes being used to locate food and detect enemies. The more primitive forms have domed shells while the more advanced forms have spiral shells, although slugs have abandoned their shells.

The bivalves are so called because they possess two parts (valves) to their shells. These can be closed together to provide protection for the mollusk inside. Bivalve mollusks include

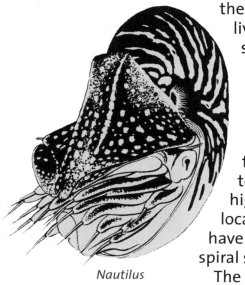

Nautilus

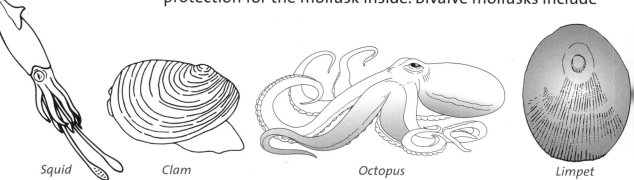

Squid   Clam   Octopus   Limpet

Snail
The shells of snails first evolved as protection from predators.

mussels, scallops, clams, cockles, oysters, and piddocks. A few species can propel themselves with jets of water, but most are adapted for burrowing or fixing themselves to objects on the sea floor.

Another phylum—Brachiopoda—includes creatures similar to the bivalves. They are known as lamp shells, because their two shells (valves) typically make a shape similar to a Roman terracotta oil lamp.

Mollusks
These creatures have succeeded in colonizing salt water, fresh water, and also terrestrial habitats, although their ancestors all lived in the sea.

IT'S A FACT
Of all invertebrates, the cephalopod mollusks include the most intelligent, and the largest species. They include octopuses, squid, cuttlefish, and nautiluses. The fossil record shows that cephalopods with coiled shells (ammonites), and straight shells (belemnites), were extremely abundant in the world's oceans until 65 million years ago. One living species with a true shell is the nautilus (*Nautilus macromphalus*). Other species have adapted it as an internal skeleton, or abandoned it altogether.

Belemnite

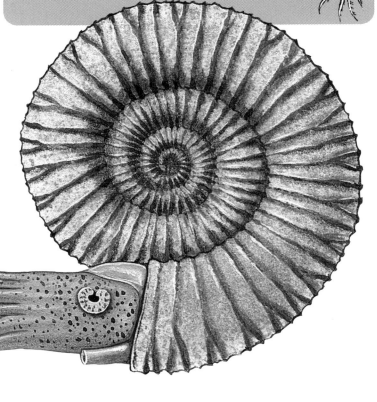

The word "arthropod" translates as "jointed foot." This is because arthropods typically possess limbs that are articulated with hinged joints. This is an evolutionary adaptation that enables them to move, despite having exoskeletons.

ARTHROPODS HAVE MANAGED to colonize habitats on land as well as in water, but water is the environment in which they first evolved. Indeed, many terrestrial arthropods, particularly insects, are actually semi-aquatic because they have larval stages that live in water. The key classes of animal in the aquatic arthropod group are: Xiphosura (king crabs); Pycnogonida (sea spiders); Crustacea (crustaceans); and the extinct subphylum Trilobitomorpha (trilobites).

King crabs are also known as horseshoe crabs, because they have a circular carapace which conceals their limbs and looks similar to a horse's hoof, or shoe. There are five species, and all are regarded as evolutionary relics. The fossil record shows that there used to be up to a hundred species. King crabs are seabed dwellers in shallow seas.

Sea spiders are peculiar creatures because many of their organs are located inside their legs, rather than in their bodies. They consequently have very slim bodies, with disproportionately large limbs. There are about 500 species, typically found feeding on the

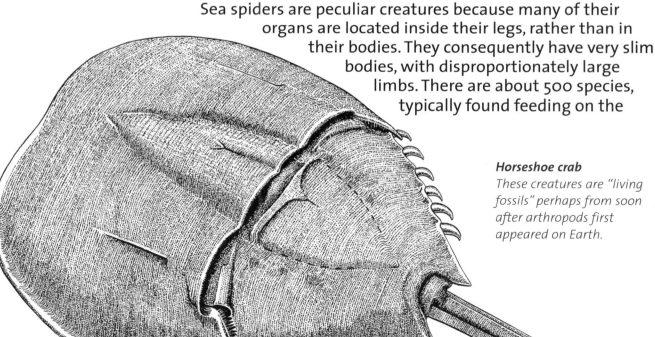

Horseshoe crab
These creatures are "living fossils" perhaps from soon after arthropods first appeared on Earth.

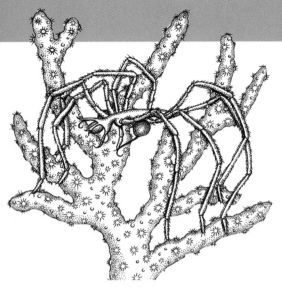

Sea spider
The spiders common on land are completely unrelated to these creatures.

soft tissues of sea anemones and similar creatures.
Crustaceans include crabs, lobsters, prawns, shrimps, krill, barnacles, slaters, woodlice, copepods, and water fleas. Although woodlice and some crabs are terrestrial to varying degrees, the rest live in marine or freshwater habitats. Clearly the class contains a great variety of forms and sizes of creature, making it impossible to describe a typical kind. However, they all have two pairs of antennae, and most species possess a carapace (body shell) and gills with which they extract oxygen from water.

BACK IN TIME
Trilobites were abundant until the Permian period—290 million to 248 million years ago. Some 15,000 species have been identified from the fossil record. Naturally, with so many species, they varied greatly in size and form. Their common features included head, thorax, and pygidium ("tail") and two lengthwise grooves giving the body a three-lobed appearance.

Trilobite

Lobster

Crab

© DIAGRAM

The arthropods include the first animals that adapted to truly terrestrial environments, where habitats were dry and desiccation was a danger. They were able to do this because they possessed impermeable exoskeletons, which prevented loss of moisture from the animals.

THERE ARE EIGHT CLASSES of arthropod that are essentially terrestrial, although they often include members that are aquatic for at least part of their lives. They are: Arachnida (spiders, mites, and scorpions); Chilopoda (centipedes); Crustacea (woodlice and crabs); Diplopoda (millipedes); Insecta (beetles, bugs, grasshoppers, dragonflies, moths, etc.); Onychophora (velvet worms); Pauropoda (pauropods); and Symphyla (symphylans).

The velvet worms are the most primitive. They have soft bodies and look like a cross between a caterpillar and a worm. The fossil record shows that they once lived in water, so it seems likely that they represent a transitional phase leading to the centipedes, millipedes, pauropods and symphylans, which all share a similar body plan. They all have elongated bodies made from segments, with one or two pairs of legs per segment.

Moths
These insects are representative of those that hatch in a larval form, often known as caterpillars or grubs.

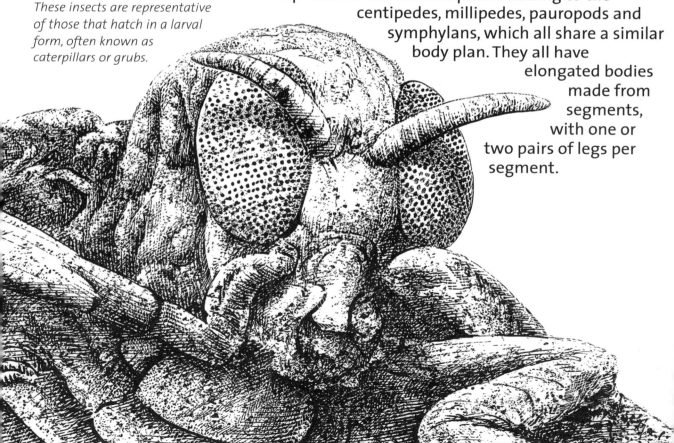

Most crustaceans are aquatic but some crabs have adapted to life on land in their adult form. The only truly terrestrial crustaceans are woodlice. They have achieved this by laying eggs in which the larvae develop into miniature versions of the adults, which are called nymphs, before hatching.

This same technique is used in insects and arachnids, although many insects still hatch in a larval form. Insects and arachnids are generally very similar to one another, but there are two obvious design characteristics that mark them apart. Adult insects have three parts to their bodies: head, thorax, and abdomen. Arachnids have just two parts to their bodies. Instead of having a separate head and thorax, they are fused together to form a cephalothorax, which is then attached to the abdomen. Insects have three pairs of legs, while arachnids have four pairs.

IT'S A FACT
To compensate for their relative lack of body flexibility—as they have a fused head and thorax—arachnids are equipped with up to four pairs of eyes, which are often mounted on a turret, to provide all-round visibility.

Classes of arthropod

Arachnids

Crustaceans

Insects

Velvet worms

Centipedes

Millipedes

Pauropods

Symphylans

Spiders
Although similar to insects, these are quite a different group of creatures.

The echinoderms include starfishes, sea urchins, sand dollars, and sea cucumbers.

AT FIRST SIGHT THESE ANIMALS might seem very different from one another, but appearances can be deceptive. In fact, they all share a similar basic body plan and other characteristics. Most other animals possess bilateral symmetry which means that they are divided into two halves down a center line, so that each half is a mirror image of the other. Echinoderms possess radial symmetry instead. This means that they are divided into similar sections like slices of cake. There are typically five sections, but some species have many more.

If a starfish is regarded as the basic design, then it is possible to see how the other forms have evolved. In the case of the sea urchin, the arms have been folded upward to create the spherical body shape. In the case of the sea cucumber, the sea urchin shape has been further modified, by elongating it into a cucumberlike shape. In the case of the sand dollar, the

Echinoderms
Radial, rather than bilateral, symmetry is a characteristic of these creatures.

Sand dollar

Star fish

Brittle star

arms of the starfish have been flattened out to form a disk shape.

Echinoderms move about with the use of tube feet, which are elastic tentacles. They have hundreds of these tube feet, which work in unison so that the animals appear to glide over the seabed where they live. The skin of echinoderms often includes plates of calcium carbonate, which give the animals some structural support as well as protection from predators, although many species are also equipped with protective spines. It is apparent that the calcium carbonate plates are the forerunner to the endoskeletons seen in vertebrates, because vertebrate bones are made from calcium carbonate and collagen. None of the living echinoderms can be seen as an evolutionary link though, because vertebrates all possess bilateral symmetry. However, the larvae of echinoderms do possess bilateral symmetry.

STRANGE BUT TRUE

Echinoderms do not have heads, due to their radial symmetry. Instead, they have a central mouth, and pass food to it with their tube feet. Many species graze on animals and plants that encrust rock surfaces, but starfish actively hunt shellfish.

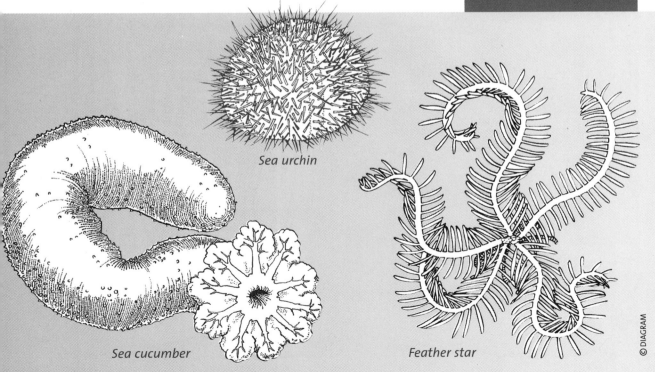

Sea urchin

Sea cucumber

Feather star

© DIAGRAM

With radial symmetry, echinoderms lack a head, which in turn means that they have no central nervous system. This changed with the evolution of the lower chordates, where bilateral symmetry became the adult body plan.

CREATURES THAT ARE bilaterally symmetrical have a nervous system that is aggregated to form a nerve cord—which is how the chordates derive their name. The chordates belong to a single phylum, called Chordata, but the lower chordates belong to two subphyla: Urochordata and Cephalochordata. The first contains the sea squirts or tunicates, while the second contains the lancelets.

The sea squirts come in sedentary and free-swimming forms, and look a bit like the polyps

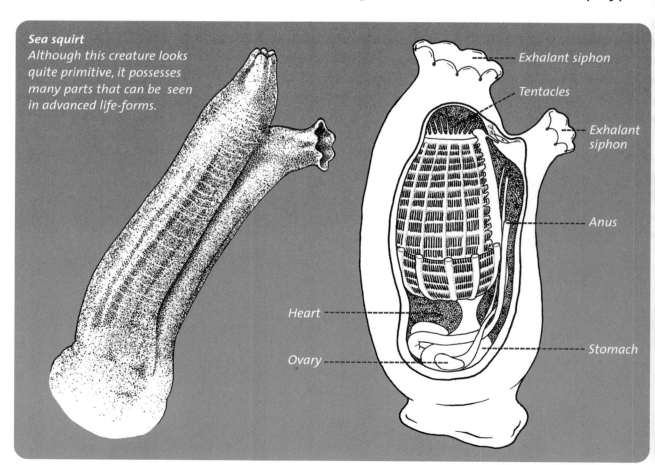

Sea squirt
Although this creature looks quite primitive, it possesses many parts that can be seen in advanced life-forms.

Exhalant siphon

Tentacles

Exhalant siphon

Anus

Heart

Ovary

Stomach

and medusas of the coelenterate group, but they lack the external rings of tentacles around the mouth. Instead, some have an internal ring of tentacles, which filter particles of food as they suck seawater in and out of their bodies. The nerve cord is always present in the larval stage of sea squirts, and is accompanied by a skeletal support rod of cartilage called the notochord.

Lancelets are more advanced than sea squirts. They resemble eels, but they lack fins and a head. There are fourteen species and all dwell at the bottom of marine habitats. Most species burrow into the substrate for protection from predators, but they can actively swim when necessary. They have rows of muscles along the body for this purpose, called myotomes. Running along the back, the nerve cord is supported by a sturdy notochord beneath it. Above the nerve cord there is a spinelike ridge called the fin ray box.

Lancelets filter particles of food with their mouths. These particles then pass through a digestive system before exiting through an anus at the other end of their bodies.

IT'S A FACT
Lancelets clearly demonstrate how the higher chordates evolved. The basic components that led to their evolution are present, so it was then a relatively simple step to the *vertebrates*, which include fishes, amphibians, reptiles, birds, and mammals.

Lancelet
This fishlike creature represents the basic blueprint for the evolution of vertebrates.

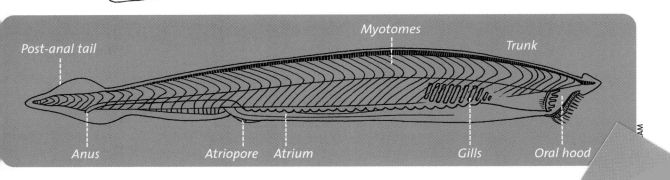

Post-anal tail · Anus · Atriopore · Atrium · Myotomes · Trunk · Gills · Oral hood

There are three fundamental reasons why organisms require nourishment. First, they need additional materials to grow. Second, they need food to metabolize into energy. Third, they need extra materials to be able to produce offspring.

PLANTS DERIVE much of their nutrition from water in the ground and carbon dioxide in the air. This is because most of the molecules that make up plants are carbohydrates, such as cellulose, which comprise the elements carbon, oxygen, and hydrogen. The rest of the nutrition they need comes from minerals dissolved in the water around their roots, such as nitrate and potassium salts.

Animals are more complex than plants and require a greater variety of nutrients. Broadly speaking, there are three kinds of animal, in terms of their feeding preferences. Herbivores eat plant matter, carnivores eat other animals, and omnivores eat both plants and animals. In fact, most animals are really omnivores, since they eat varying degrees of plant and animal matter even if they have adapted to specialized diets. If they didn't they would

A foodweb
Primary, secondary and tertiary consumers all play their part in food chains and food webs.

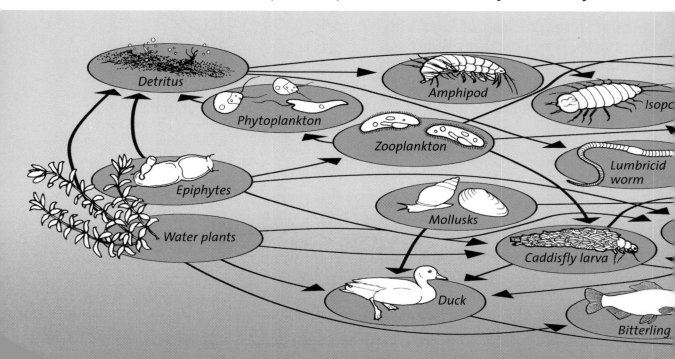

Detritus

Phytoplankton

Amphipod

Isopo

Zooplankton

Lumbricid worm

Epiphytes

Mollusks

Water plants

Caddisfly larva

Duck

Bitterling

find it very difficult to obtain the range of nutrients required to keep them alive. For example, carnivores such as foxes supplement their diet of meat with berries and leaves. Similarly herbivores such as deer supplement their diet of foliage by eating caterpillars and aphids.

Omnivores, such as badgers and bears, benefit by finding it easier to locate food at all times of the year. Other animals often have to migrate to find sufficient food supplies, or hibernate while food is unavailable.

IT'S A FACT
Humans are omnivores. We eat a variety of plant and animal foodstuffs. When we swallow our food it is broken down by stomach acid, and digested by chemicals called enzymes before being absorbed into our bodies. After all the nutrition has been removed, the waste is discarded from our digestive systems as feces. Other waste substances are removed from our blood by the kidneys and expelled in the form of urine. The name given to the separation and expulsion of metabolized waste products from the body is "excretion."

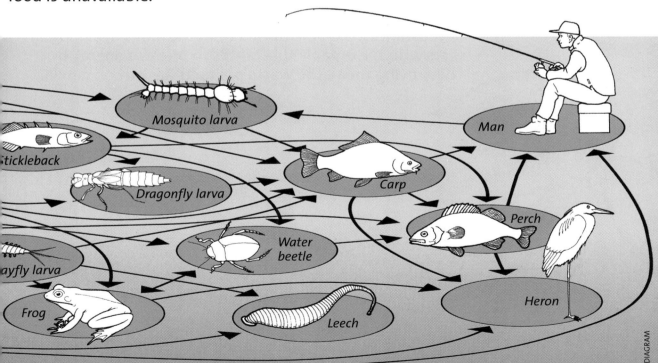

Mosquito larva

Stickleback

Dragonfly larva

Man

Carp

Perch

Water beetle

Mayfly larva

Frog

Leech

Heron

© DIAGRAM

Metabolism is the term used to describe the chemical processes that occur inside organisms to maintain life.

THERE ARE TWO GENERAL TYPES of metabolism: constructive and destructive. Constructive metabolism is where simple compounds are used to make complex molecules, such as sugars, fats, and proteins. Destructive metabolism is where complex molecules are broken down into simple compounds, some of which are used in constructive metabolism, and the rest expelled from the organism as waste matter.

In plants the principal metabolic process is photosynthesis. The green pigment, chlorophyll, uses the energy from sunlight to synthesize food from water and carbon dioxide. In photosynthesis the water is converted into its components of hydrogen and oxygen. The hydrogen is then combined with carbon dioxide to construct carbohydrate molecules, while the spare oxygen is expelled.

In animals the principal metabolic process is respiration. Respiration is the oxidation of complex organic substances. Oxygen, carried from the lungs in blood cells, reacts with the organic substances to produce energy by destroying them. The waste products are carbon dioxide

Green leaves
Chlorophyll is the green pigment in leaves that uses light energy from the Sun.

Sun

Photosynthesis
This is the process by which plants manufacture food.

IT'S A FACT
Secondary metabolic processes in animals include the synthesis of protein and fat molecules. Respiration is a *destructive* metabolic process, while molecule synthesis is a *constructive* metabolic process. Protein molecules are constructed from simpler molecules called amino acids. Fats are chains of hydrocarbon molecules which are used as a means of storing food.

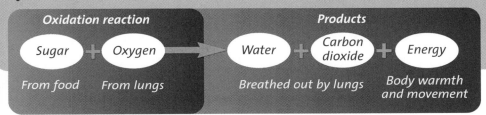

Oxidation reaction		Products		
Sugar + Oxygen →		Water +	Carbon dioxide +	Energy
From food From lungs		Breathed out by lungs		Body warmth and movement

and water. The energy produced is used to keep the animal sufficiently warm to continue with other chemical processes around the body, such as digesting foodstuffs, building new cells, and keeping the muscles working.

Metabolism is a cycle. Without food and oxygen, animals would be unable to perform respiration, yet without respiration they would be unable to digest food and breathe. The absence of one component will lead to the death of an organism because the cycle has been broken. For this reason, organisms are equipped with senses and warning systems that are designed to prevent the cycle being broken if at all possible. In fact, all life would have ceased to exist if these mechanisms had not evolved to be as effective as they are.

Respiration (below)
Crickets (below left) are equipped with holes in their abdomens, called spiracles, for breathing oxygen from the air. Instead of spiracles, spiders (below right) have chambers with booklike layers of tissue for absorbing oxygen.

The spiracle of a cricket

The "lung" of a spider

© DIAGRAM

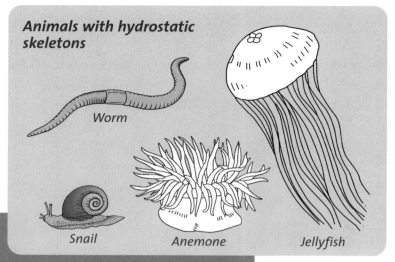

Animals with hydrostatic skeletons

Worm

Snail

Anemone

Jellyfish

Animals and plants need ways of supporting and protecting themselves physically. The cell wall is the most basic form of protection, acting both as a bag to hold the contents of the cell in one place, and giving it three-dimensional shape. This is true of any cell, whether it is the whole organism or is simply one of millions comprising a larger organism.

Mayfly
This is a primitive insect which possesses an external skeleton.

AS MANY PRIMITIVE LIFE-FORMS are aquatic, they have avoided the need for a rigid skeleton, relying instead on cell pressure to keep their shape. This is called hydrostatics.

Physical support started to become an engineering problem when animals began to require means of locomotion over the surfaces of ocean floors and through the substrate. Worms were the pioneers by evolving a system of longitudinal and concentric muscles capable of peristalsis—the sending of pulses along the body as a means of propulsion. Mollusks developed similar ways of moving, but the best solution was to have a rigid structure on which to anchor muscles, and to provide the leverage necessary for limbs. Arthropods and echinoderms both evolved species that possessed exoskeletons, a skeleton outside of the body, to support themselves in this way.

In the case of the arthropods the entire body became encased in a tough exoskeleton. This was perfect for supporting their internal workings, and for attaching muscles. However, it also meant that the body had to be divided into sections, articulated with joints, and that each animal had to shed its exoskeleton periodically in order to grow. For this reason the arthropods have remained largely unchanged for millions of years as they have little capacity to evolve into higher life forms.

Lobster
This body armor is an example of the extremes to which an external skeleton can be taken.

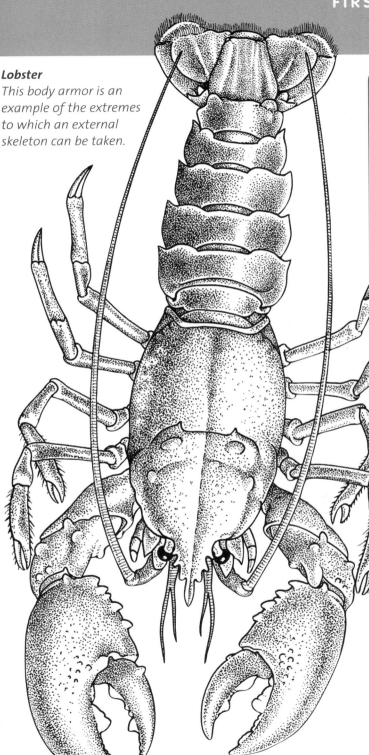

IT'S A FACT
The endoskeleton, such as that in humans, proved to be the optimum solution for higher life-forms, because it has a double purpose. On the one hand, it provides a scaffoldlike frame for supporting the muscles and organs of the body, as well as allowing continued growth without having to shed the skin. On the other hand, it protects the most important parts of the body. For example, the ribcage protects the lungs and heart; the skull protects the brain; and the vertebral column protects the spinal cord.

Squid
Squid have slight skeletons, called quills, in their bodies. Otherwise they rely on hydrostatics to maintain their shape.

© DIAGRAM

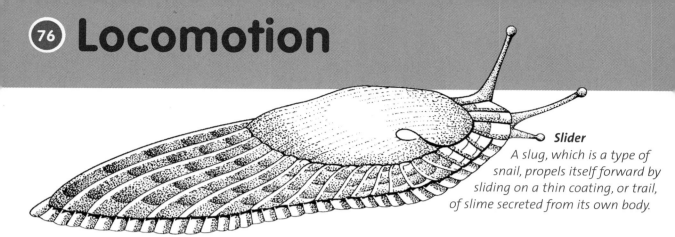

Slider
A slug, which is a type of snail, propels itself forward by sliding on a thin coating, or trail, of slime secreted from its own body.

The earliest forms of locomotion developed to allow movement through water. Some simple animals possess hairlike structures called cilia which vibrate in waves like tiny oars. Others have wiggling tails, or pulse their bodies to create movement.

MOLLUSKS EVOLVED two important means of locomotion in water. First came the water jet and, secondly, fins and streamlining, which have proven their efficiency by becoming ubiquitous among fishes and other aquatic vertebrates, although these features evolved quite separately in these groups.

Worms became the first animals to master burrowing locomotion, with the use of muscles inside a flexible but non-elastic skin, called a hydrostatic skeleton. A similar principle was developed in the muscular foot of gastropods as they adapted to traveling on surfaces underwater and on land. In echinoderms tube feet evolved to move the animals by gliding them over surfaces. In arthropods, combinations of muscles and limbs became used for locomotion in aquatic and terrestrial environments, and it was the walking insects that

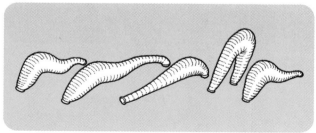

Looping leeches
When moving on a surface, leeches use suckers at both ends to "walk."

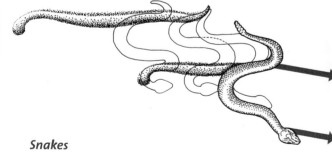

Snakes
Having no legs, snakes have evolved ways of moving by sending muscular waves along the length of their bodies.

became the first animals to master aerial locomotion, or flight.

Some of the larger flying insects have wings that achieve true flight, in the sense that they have an airfoil cross-section, thereby creating lift with forward motion. This is demonstrated in their ability to glide, as is seen in certain butterflies and dragonflies. Most insect wings do not achieve flight in this way, however, but rely instead on complex movements that operate the wings in a similar way to the oars of a boat. As a result they can possess relatively small wings, but they require huge flight muscles to provide the strength needed to achieve flight.

Forward rotation

Backward rotation

Bees (left)
Most insects cannot simply glide on their wings, but rely instead on complex movements to create the lift they need to fly.

Muscular movement
Whatever the engineering involved in achieving movement, animals rely on muscles to provide the necessary mechanical forces.

Vertebrate

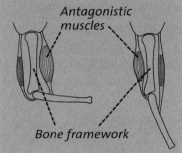

Antagonistic muscles

Bone framework

Arthropod

Antagonistic muscles

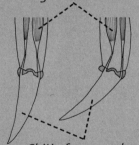

Chitin framework

Worm

Locomotive pulse

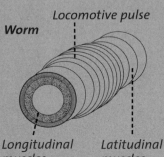

Longitudinal muscles

Latitudinal muscles

© DIAGRAM

IT'S A FACT

An important principle of locomotion, which can be seen in animals with either exoskeletons or endoskeletons, is that of antagonistic muscles. This means that a limb or wing has two sets of muscles that work in opposition to one another. One set is used to extend the limb (extensor muscles) while the other set is used to retract the limb (retractor muscles). For the system to work properly a rigid, jointed skeleton is required to provide mechanical leverage.

For the very smallest marine creatures, such as single-celled organisms and invertebrate larvae, orientation and navigation are not of great importance, as they tend to drift about with the currents as a single mass of zooplankton.

KNOWING WHICH WAY IS UP, and which way is down, is important because many planktonic animals migrate between the surface waters and the depths of the sea in a daily cycle. The key stimulants are the light and warmth of the Sun, which signals to the creatures both where the surface is, and what time of day it is. These animals also possess neutral buoyancy to enable them to move up and down with a certain degree of ease.

With larger aquatic invertebrates the sense organs tend to become more advanced. The eyes are capable of accurate interpretation of the environment, and touch becomes an important means of navigation. Animals can therefore see and feel their way around their habitats. Many aquatic invertebrates migrate seasonally because of changes in the weather above the surface that affect the oceans. They travel away from coastal areas to deeper waters, where conditions remain stabilized. Changes in light levels, temperature, and water pressure play key roles in telling them

Plankton
There are two types of plankton: zooplankton comprises tiny animals, and phytoplankton, tiny plants.

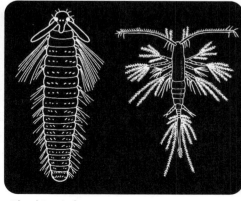

Planktonic larva   Planktonic copepod

where to go, because the ocean floor typically falls away as they travel farther from land.

For terrestrial invertebrates the rules change considerably, because life in the air is very different. Gravity is a more obvious factor for telling which way is up, but light levels do not necessarily indicate direction as clearly. In moisture-loving creatures, darkness and humidity are sought: animals such as worms, slugs, and snails know to avoid bright and dry environments.

DID YOU KNOW?
When male moths search for females they navigate by sight and smell. Male moths have feathery antennae that detect perfume emitted by females. When they notice the scent they lock onto the flight direction by keeping the image of the Moon fixed in one position in their eyes, and making slight visual adjustments as they go.

Incidentally, moths encircle light bulbs because they confuse them with the Moon and try to keep the light source in a fixed position.

Brine shrimp
This is one of the many thousands of types of creature that comprise zooplankton.

Hawk moth

© DIAGRAM

Animals need to communicate, mainly so that they can reproduce successfully. Communication is also important in protection from enemies, and to tell each other where to find sources of food.

FOR LOWER LIFE-FORMS, one of the most important messages to relay to other animals is what species it is, and then which sex. Visual signals do not necessarily perform this function very well, so invertebrates employ a variety of other communication techniques. Some male spiders, for example, use nuptial gifts of food to tempt a female. Courtship in moths is accompanied by the release of particular chemicals that attract mates. If the other animal responds in the appropriate way then the courtship ritual can move on to the next phase, until copulation occurs.

For many animals, congregating in large numbers is an effective means of deterring predators. This is because predators tend to get confused by the sight of many individual animals moving as one. To make sure that this strategy works effectively, prey animals need to stay in constant communication with one another. If they stray from the

Spiders
Male spiders have to be sure that they communicate with females in exactly the right way to avoid being eaten while attempting to mate.

Pheromone detectors
The featherlike antennae of male moths are designed to filter pheromone molecules from the air.

swarm or shoal, then they are far more likely to be picked off by a predator.

Some animals frighten off their enemies by signaling that they are something that they are not. For example, many flies mimic the appearance of wasps, so that birds will not attempt to eat them. The wasps themselves are brightly colored to warn birds against trying to eat them, because the birds will be injured by a sting.

IT'S A FACT
If an animal locates a food source that is far too plentiful for its own requirements, it makes sense to inform others of its own species so that they can all benefit from the bounty. A good example of this is seen in honeybees. When a worker bee finds a source of nectar and pollen, it flies straight back to the nest and performs a dance to communicate the direction and distance to fly.

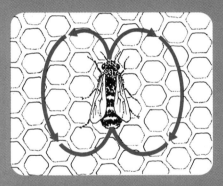

Honeybee dance
Worker honeybees cannot speak, so they use special dances to describe the locations of feeding sites to their sister bees.

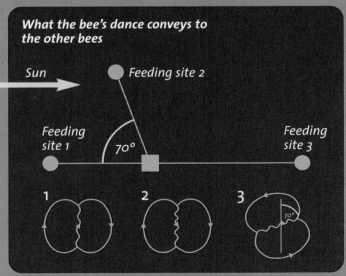

What the bee's dance conveys to the other bees

Sun   Feeding site 2

Feeding site 1   70°   Feeding site 3

1   2   3   70°

Although most vertebrates reproduce sexually, there are other ways of multiplying that are seen in invertebrates.

IN VERY SIMPLE ANIMALS, such as hydras, new individuals can grow from outgrowths on the body of the parent. This process is called budding. In aphids, females can reproduce by parthenogenesis. The term translates as "virgin creation" because it means reproduction from an ovum or egg without fertilization by sperm—a form of asexual reproduction. The eggs develop into miniature adults. Budding and parthenogenesis are quicker than sexual reproduction but can take place only when conditions are favorable. However, these offspring are clones of their parents, so they have identical genes. For this reason, hydras and aphids also reproduce sexually at the end of the growing season to ensure that the population has sufficient genetic variety to allow natural selection to work.

Many invertebrates are hermaphrodites. This means they have both male and female sexual organs—they are monoecious. Examples are earthworms and snails. They seldom mate with themselves, but can mate with any individual from their own species, and don't have to search for an individual of the opposite sex. This strategy offers the advantage of saving time, yet it still ensures genetic variety in a species. Invertebrates with separate sexes are described as dioecious. Although hermaphrodites would seem to have the better reproductive strategy, dioecious species actually

Hydra
This animal is reproducing by creating a smaller copy of itself from a bud on its side.

Spider
This female spider is carrying a ball of fertilized eggs inside a silk cocoon.

DID YOU KNOW
Sexual reproduction is where a male and female supply germ cells, called gametes. The male gamete is called a spermatozoon (sperm) and the female gamete is called an ovum (egg). The sperm fertilizes the egg to form a zygote cell, which shares the genes of both gametes. The zygote then divides to form an embryo, which develops into offspring.

benefit from increased genetic variety. This is because males and females can vary considerably in shape and size within a species. Also, when forced to invest more effort into finding a mate it means that individuals are likely to travel farther and bring genes from different populations, rather than remain local.

Damselflies
When these insects pair off, they adopt a "wheel" position so that the female can receive the sperm packet of the male.

©DIAGRAM

An important characteristic of invertebrates is that they develop into adult form via larval stages. This is not exclusive to them, as vertebrates such as fish and amphibians also have larvae. Larvae can be very different from the adult form, both in shape and size.

MARINE INVERTEBRATES typically produce larvae that live as part of the oceanic plankton. They remain like this until they develop into small versions of the adults and begin to adopt the adult lifestyle, whatever that may be. Crustaceans, coelenterates, and echinoderms all have these planktonic larvae.

In terrestrial, or land-dwelling, invertebrates the larvae need to be adapted to life out of water, so they are more advanced when they hatch from their eggs. Insects are good examples. They are broadly divided into two groups, depending on the way their larvae develop. Many hatch essentially as miniature versions of the adults, having completed some of their development within the egg itself. They are called nymphs, and they gradually grow into adults by a process of development called incomplete metamorphosis. Examples are grasshoppers, crickets, mantids, cockroaches, and true bugs. Other terrestrial arthropods, such as spiders, millipedes, centipedes, and woodlice, also develop by

Complete metamorphosis
The caterpillar, pupa, and adult insect all look very different from one another, reflecting the complete change which occurs at each stage of development.

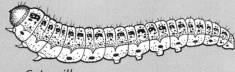

Caterpillar

Pupa

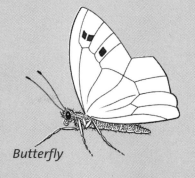

Butterfly

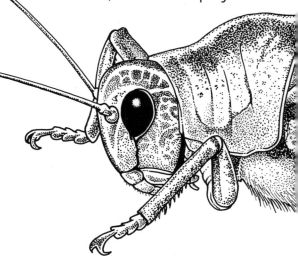

incomplete metamorphosis. Soft-bodied, terrestrial invertebrates, such as worms, snails, and slugs simply develop by growing bigger until they mature, for they do not shed their skins to grow, as arthropods do.

The other type of insect has larvae that are completely different to the adult form—variously called grubs, maggots, worms, or caterpillars. When they are fully grown they change into adults by a process called complete metamorphosis, which involves an intermediate stage called a pupa (plural: pupae) or chrysalis, in which the components of the animal are dramatically rearranged. Examples are beetles, bees, ants, wasps, butterflies, moths, and true flies.

IT'S A FACT
In the case of aquatic insects, their larvae are divided in the same way as terrestrial insects. This is because they evolved on land before adapting to freshwater habitats. For example, water bugs develop by incomplete metamorphosis, while water beetles develop by complete metamorphosis.

Incomplete metamorphosis
Members of the grasshopper family grow by a process of incomplete change. A young locust is a small wingless version of the adult.

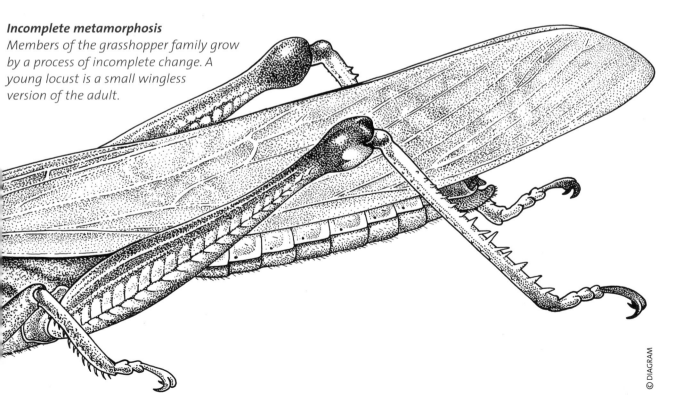

© DIAGRAM

All invertebrates are adapted to obtain food and to avoid becoming the food of other animals. These are known as strategies of offense and defense.

I N THE CASE OF herbivorous (plant-eating) invertebrates, offense involves beating the defenses of the plants they eat. For the most part, plants manage to survive by producing more foliage than they actually need, but many also protect themselves with poisonous sap or bristles that make it difficult for invertebrates to feed on their leaves and stems in the first place. Equally important to herbivorous invertebrates is their own defense against carnivorous invertebrates and vertebrates alike, which would happily eat them. Means of defense include armor, weapons, camouflage, and mimicking dangerous invertebrates, as well as speed and stealth.

Carnivorous (animal-eating) invertebrates use many of the same defenses as herbivorous species, because they, too, may become prey to other animals. However, they are also equipped with the weapons and tools they need for catching, attacking, killing, and eating their own prey. These may include formidable pincers for seizing animals or impressive fangs for piercing their bodies. They may also be armed with the means of delivering powerful stings or poisonous bites, which are doubly useful for defense. Some carnivorous invertebrates actively hunt their prey, while others use traps to catch them or lie ready to ambush unsuspecting animals as they pass by.

Predator
Even tree trunks do not always provide a safe haven for beetle grubs from parasitoid wasps.

Tsetse fly
Female tsetse flies give birth to single, fully-grown, grubs. This strategy improves the offspring's chances of survival.

IT'S A FACT

Offense and defense have been integral components of the design and behavior of organisms from very early on in the story of evolution. This phenomenon is described as the biological arms race. The analogy alludes to human warfare, in which enemies are continually forced to improve their arms technology to prevent them losing a war. Since strategies for offense and defense can never be completely effective, invertebrates universally use the backup strategy of multiplying as much as possible to ensure that some of their species will survive no matter what.

Stag beetles

Hercules beetle

Assassin bug
Efficient killers, these insects are equipped with piercing mouth parts that enable them to suck the life out of their victims.

© DIAGRAM

For invertebrates, their most fundamental senses are concerned with locating and recognizing food sources. To do this, many rely mainly on their senses of taste and smell.

TASTING AND SMELLING are essentially the same function, because they involve the detection of a substance's molecules, either on its surface or released into air or water. For this reason, they are collectively known as "chemoreception," since they work on a chemical level.

Invertebrates do not have noses and tongues for smelling and tasting as such mammals as humans do. Instead, they have chemoreceptors located in the most appropriate areas of their bodies. Leeches, for example, taste chemicals in water through their skin and will immediately respond if they detect a potential food source. Medicinal leeches feed on the blood of mammals, while other leeches may feed on the blood of birds, amphibians, fish, or

Annelid nervous system
The nerves finally divide into a fine matrix at the surface of the worm's skin.

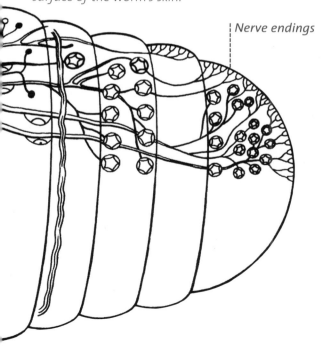

Nerve endings

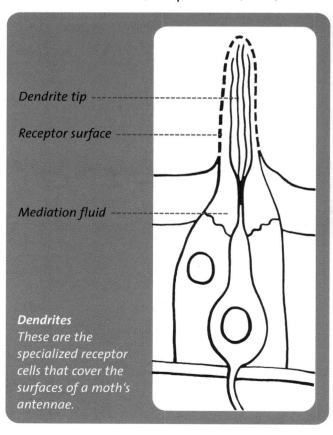

Dendrite tip ------

Receptor surface ------

Mediation fluid ------

Dendrites
These are the specialized receptor cells that cover the surfaces of a moth's antennae.

invertebrates. Each food source has its own distinctive flavor.

In the case of insects, they taste things with their feet. This is because their feet are the first things to make contact with surfaces and their eyes are usually angled to look upward, not downward. Besides, it would not necessarily be easy for an insect to judge a food source—such as the nectar in flowers—by sight. Insects also smell the air with their feelers or antennae. Good examples are male moths, which can follow the faint scent trails of females over several miles. They have featherlike antennae designed for filtering scent molecules from the air.

DID YOU KNOW?

Invertebrates also taste and smell their environment for things that are potentially harmful. For example, ants need to know whether other ants they encounter are from the same colony as themselves or from another, especially if a food source requires gathering and defending. They do this by running their antennae over another ant's head and thorax to detect its odor. Even ants of the same species have subtly different odors if they come from different colonies. If the odor is a match with their own, then a greeting gesture is made. If not, then a fight may break out.

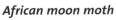

African moon moth
The male moth's antennae are covered in dendrites for detecting the scent of female moths.

© DIAGRAM

Invertebrates have developed a number of organs for balance and coordination, so that they can move around safely.

ON THE MOST BASIC LEVEL, it is useful for invertebrates to know which way is up and which way is down. Having established this, they can then tell the nature of their own position and movements in relation to their surroundings.

Cephalopods (octopuses, squid, and cuttlefish) have an arrangement called the statocyst, located near the brain. Part of the statocyst comprises a fluid-filled sac, in which there is a calcium carbonate lump called the macula. The macula is attached to the ends of a group of horizontal hairlike fibers that are extremely sensitive to position. Gravity affects the macula as the animal changes position, so that the fibers tell the brain which way the animal is oriented in relation to the upright position. The other part of the statocyst is called the crista. It comprises a belt of cells that correspond with the vertical, longitudinal, and transverse planes. The cells possess weighted flaps, sensitive to movement, so that the animal can feel the effects of acceleration, pitching, and rolling as it swims.

Cuttlefish
These cephalopods are predators of crabs. They rely on an organ called a statocyst to provide the accurate coordination required for successful hunting.

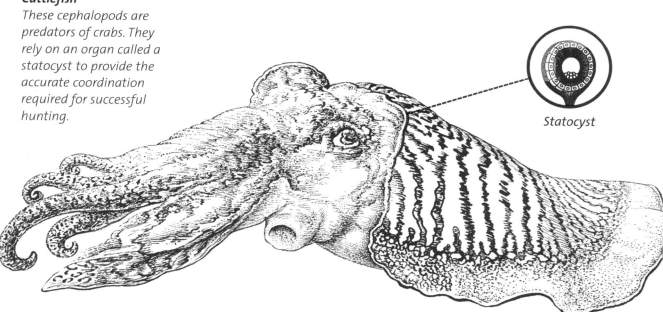

Statocyst

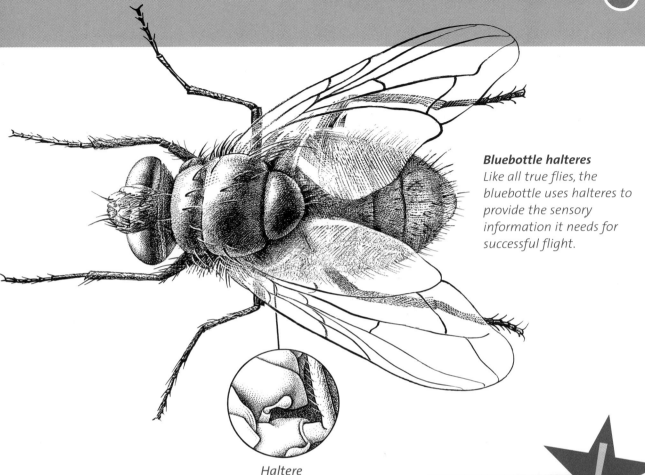

Bluebottle halteres
Like all true flies, the bluebottle uses halteres to provide the sensory information it needs for successful flight.

Haltere

Flying insects use a different principle altogether for their balance and coordination. They have a system of gauges located at their wing bases. These measure the relative forces by the strain exerted on them as the insect moves through the air. This is best seen in true flies, which have their rear pair of wings atrophied into small clublike organs called halteres. The halteres oscillate in flight so that their weighted ends produce a gyroscopic effect and feed the central nervous system with the information it needs to keep the insect airborne. Indeed, a fly without halteres will spiral out of control, as will a cephalopod lacking its statocyst.

IT'S A FACT
"Kinesthetics" is the term used for an animal's awareness of the position of its own body parts in relation to one another. This works by the animal possessing a kind of mental map of its body, so that the angle of its joints tell it what posture it is in.

© DIAGRAM

In evolution, eyes started off as nothing more than photosensitive cells arranged to form photoreceptors.

AS THEIR NAME SUGGESTS, photoreceptors (light-receivers) are merely able to tell the difference between light levels. This enabled invertebrates to judge whether it might be night or day, or whether they might be safely hidden or dangerously exposed. Earthworms, for example, have simple eyes placed all over their bodies so that they can tell whether any part of them is above ground.

More complex eyes evolved in invertebrates in the form of compound eyes. They derived their name because they comprise clusters of photoreceptive cells compounded together as a single eye. Each cell supplies its own information so that a visual image is made up from a collection of dots, just like the pixels on a television screen or a computer monitor. The creature then interprets the dots to form a whole image.

These image-forming eyes have evolved in different invertebrate groups independently of one another. However, they fall into two general types, as it seems that there are two

Crab eyes
The eyes of a crab are mounted on flexible stalks to improve its vision.

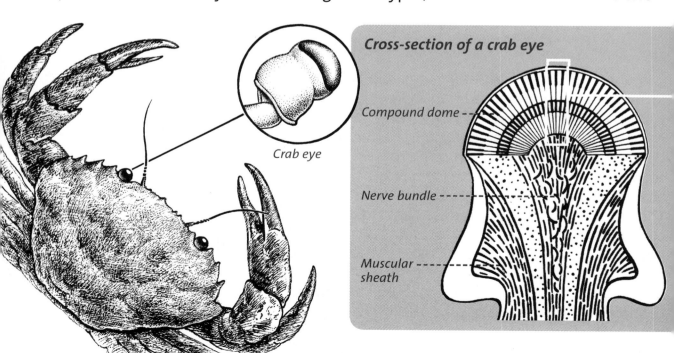

Crab eye

Cross-section of a crab eye

Compound dome

Nerve bundle

Muscular sheath

fundamental ways that eyes can evolve, based on the scientific principles they use. There are those with a fixed-focus lens in front of each photoreceptive cell, and there are those with just one variable-focus lens held in front of a cup of photoreceptive cells. The first type of eye is the more primitive, being unable to adjust focus, but it is ubiquitous among insects, which make up a large proportion of invertebrates. The second type is seen in mollusks and spiders, although the specific designs vary considerably, having evolved from different points of origin.

IT'S A FACT

The eyes of cephalopods, such as octopuses, are very similar to those of vertebrates such as mammals, including humans. This is an example of convergent evolution, since their eyes evolved from a separate starting point. It is clear that they evolved separately because of one fundamental difference in their design— the way in which focusing is achieved. In our eyes focusing is achieved by altering the shape of the lens. In octopuses the lens is fixed, so the retina is moved back and forth instead.

Lens -----------
Retina -----------

Octopus eye

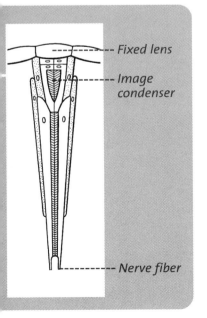

----- *Fixed lens*

----- *Image condenser*

----- *Nerve fiber*

Compound eyes
Each optical unit appears as a tiny dot, lots of which make up the surface of the eyes.

© DIAGRAM

Although we usually associate advanced forms of vision with vertebrates, it should be noted that some invertebrates also have remarkable visual abilities, even though they are more primitive life-forms.

STEREOSCOPIC, OR BINOCULAR, VISION involves the use of paired eyes that can view an object simultaneously. This enables an animal to interpret what it sees three-dimensionally, giving it spatial vision. With spatial vision an animal is better able to judge the size, shape, and distance of objects. This is especially useful if it happens to be a predator or if it needs to travel through foliage, for example. There are several invertebrate groups where species have their eyes positioned appropriately to achieve spatial vision. Among the insects, dragonflies use theirs to chase down other flying insects. Among the cephalopods, cuttlefishes employ theirs to stalk seabed-dwelling crustaceans. Among the arachnids, jumping spiders put theirs to lethal effect by pouncing on unsuspecting prey.

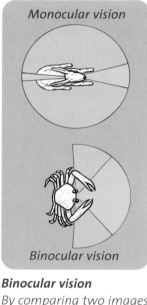

Monocular vision

Binocular vision

Binocular vision
By comparing two images of the same object, crabs can judge its distance and size far better than with one image.

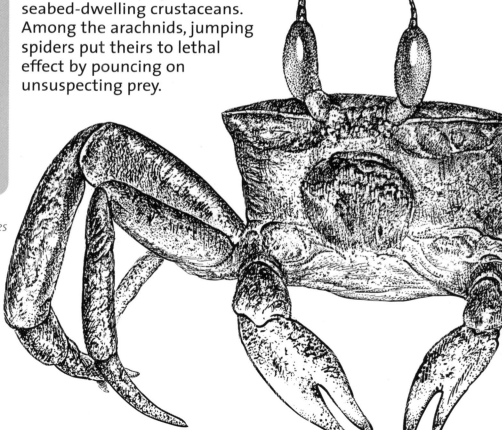

Jumping spider
Some spiders have more than two eyes looking in the same direction. This provides three-dimensional vision accurate enough to jump on flies.

Many invertebrates have color vision. This is evident from the coloration seen in groups such as butterflies. Any bright colors that are not used for other purposes—such as warning or camouflage—indicate color vision in the invertebrate species. Furthermore, invertebrates often have the ability to see colors that are invisible to the human eye. This is because light waves exist in a spectrum of electromagnetic wavelengths. The full spectrum reaches from infrared to ultraviolet, but humans can see only the middle part—what we call visible light. Having the ability to see infrared or ultraviolet wavelengths enables invertebrates to pinpoint food sources more accurately when dealing with objects that would otherwise be difficult to locate due to low light levels or confusing surroundings.

Colored patterns
Male and female butterflies identify each other by the patterns of color on their wings, which are also used in courtship display.

IT'S A FACT
Nectar-feeding insects, such as bees and butterflies, can see ultraviolet light very well. The flowers from which they feed reflect ultraviolet wavelengths from the light of the Sun, unlike leaves which absorb them. This means that the flowers stand out clearly against the background, and the insects know exactly where to aim.

© DIAGRAM

Sounds and movements generate mechanical waves through air, water, and solid objects. These are otherwise known as vibrations. Animals detect vibrations using pressure-sensitive cells, and this is the principle behind both hearing and touch.

PRESSURE-SENSITIVE CELLS detect either vibrations or direct contact with objects by the changes in pressure caused to the fluid inside them. These pressure changes generate electrical signals with strengths appropriate to the degree of stimulus. The electrical signals then send nerve impulses to the central nervous system so that the animal can read and interpret the information.

Many soft-bodied invertebrates possess touch-sensitive cells all over their bodies. These give them an ability to detect vibrations through water and soil, but they cannot hear things through air. Ears come into their own with the hard-bodied invertebrates: arthropods, particularly insects.

Insect ears are designed to funnel and amplify sound vibrations, because they are generally weaker than those traveling through liquids and solids. The ear therefore takes the form of a funnel-shaped pit, leading to a diaphragm, which vibrates and stimulates touch sensitive cells.

As arthropods have inflexible skins they are intrinsically restricted in their ability to detect movement, either in the form of vibrations or direct contact. However, they have gotten around this problem by enhancing touch sensitivity in their

Early warning
Earwigs sense the vibrations of predators through their feet. They usually scurry into hiding places as soon as vibrations are felt.

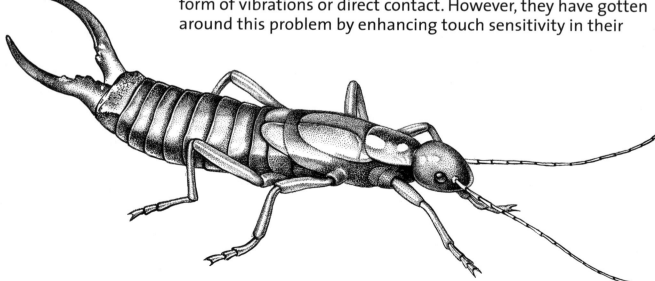

Sensing prey
The hairs on spiders' legs are especially sensitive to touch, so that they can feel the slightest movement of prey in their webs.

joints. This is best observed in orb spiders, which can detect the slightest movements of prey in their webs by using their legs. Grasshoppers and crickets have ears on their legs, so that they can be used to detect vibrations, both those in the air and those traveling along the objects on which they are standing. This gives them a much clearer idea of when a potential mate is beginning to get close enough for visual contact.

IT'S A FACT
When waves travel through water as the result of sounds or movements, they carry farther than those traveling through air or land. This is because water cannot be compressed, but can become pressurized, so that the energy is conveyed without being absorbed so readily. Aquatic invertebrates can therefore detect sounds and movements very acutely or clearly, because they are pressurized by the waves.

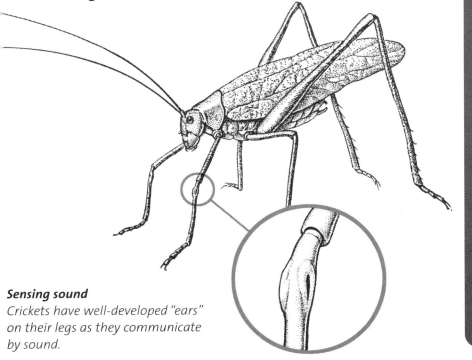

Sensing sound
Crickets have well-developed "ears" on their legs as they communicate by sound.

© DIAGRAM

Humans have five basic senses (sight, hearing, touch, taste, and smell) that are suited to a particular lifestyle. They are generally unspecialized compared to other animals, because humans have the capacity to use their intelligence and technology alongside their senses.

MANY ANIMALS HAVE SENSES far more acutely sensitive to stimuli than our own, because they are much more reliant on them for survival. Invertebrates often possess heightened or super senses, partly because they live in a micro-world, rather than a macro-world like our own. In their micro-world the stimuli for their senses tend to be far weaker in strength than those we encounter. They also have to deal with communication over proportionately long distances, and predators with highly-specialized adaptations.

Here are some examples of invertebrates with super senses. Wood wasps can detect the faintest movements of beetle grubs hidden inside tree

Echolocation (above)
This extra sense helps bats to find their way around during the night. It works like radar: high-pitched squeaks bounce off objects, and the resulting echoes enable the bats to detect what is around them.

Smell and sight (above)
Male moths search for females using feathery antennae to detect females' scents, and then lock onto their flight direction using the Moon as a guide.

Taste or smell (above)
After a period of four years at sea, a salmon returns to breed in the exact freshwater stream in which it was hatched.

Acoustic focusing (left)
Dolphins possess a melon-shaped forehead which helps to focus the echolocating sounds they produce.

branches. They do this so that they can inject the grubs with eggs using a needle-like ovipositor. The wasp larvae then eat the beetle grubs alive. Many noctuid moths can detect the ultrasonic calls of echolocating bats. This enables them to drop from the air in time to avoid being eaten by the bats. Female mosquitoes can detect the odor of mammals from several miles in their search for a blood meal. It is our feet in particular that produce the odor attractive to mosquitoes.

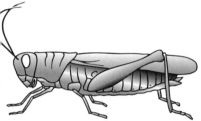

Legwork (above)
Grasshoppers "talk" to one another by rubbing their legs together.

Super smell (above)
Mosquitoes can detect the distinctive odor of mammals from a great distance away.

Emitting light (below)
Fireflies have the ability to make their presence known by emitting light. Their light organs are arranged in different patterns according to the species to which they belong.

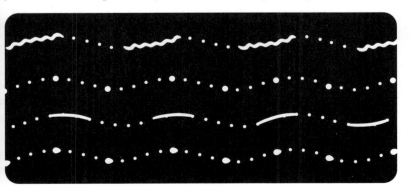

STRANGE BUT TRUE

Many invertebrates possess remarkable abilities. A number of species can emit light, called phosphorescence, by a chemical process. Fireflies and glowworms use the light to communicate with one another in darkness. By contrast, grasshoppers, crickets, and cicadas communicate with song, by day or night. Their song is actually called stridulation, and is achieved by the rubbing together of legs or wings. It works in a similar way to running a thumbnail across the teeth of a comb. A tympanic organ, rather like the skin of a drum, then amplifies the noise to many times its original volume.

Invertebrates, such as coelenterates (jellyfish, sea anemones, and coral polyps) have only simple networks of nerve cells.

M OST NERVOUS IMPULSES are weak and localized so that the whole animal is not aware of a stimulus. Nervous impulses also travel relatively slowly in coelenterates, rendering them unable to react or move quickly. Predatory species therefore rely on special stinging cells, called nematocysts, to immobilize prey animals.

In insects the nervous system is more advanced. The nerve cells are gathered together into a cord along the centerline of the body to form a central nervous system. In addition there is a

Jellyfish

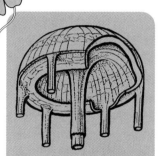

Nerve net
Nerves form a net to cover as much of the organism as possible.

Nervous systems
Although they may be arranged regularly or irregularly, the nervous systems of invertebrates are essentially designed so that they can sense their contrasting environments.

Aurelia

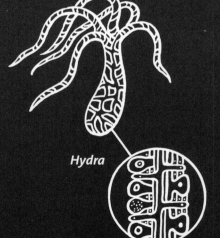
Hydra

Flatworm

series of swellings called ganglia (singular: ganglion) which are collections of nerve cells. At the head end there is a cerebral ganglion, which is a very simple brain, although each ganglion works as a brain in its own right. This is evident when insects are decapitated, for their lower bodies can function apparently unaffected for some time afterward.

Cephalopods (octopuses, squid, and cuttlefishes) have the most advanced nervous systems among the invertebrates. They possess a ring of ganglia in the head forming the brain, which is surprisingly intelligent. Captive octopuses have been shown to be capable of solving complex problems and remembering what they have learned. The nervous system in the rest of their bodies is not centralized, however, although it is symmetrical.

IT'S A FACT
The evolution of a brain is something that has occurred in various animal groups independently. The process is described as encephalization. It came into its own with the vertebrates, because the skull gave physical support and protection to such a complex organ. In humans the brain comprises some ten billion cells with thousands of billions of connecting cells called synapses. It is the single most complex organic structure known to science, and little understood as a result.

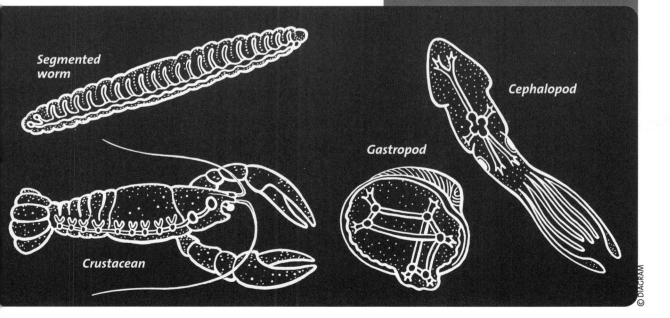

Segmented worm

Cephalopod

Gastropod

Crustacean

© DIAGRAM

One of the most fundamental and commonplace phenomena in the animal kingdom for improving survival is for species to pretend they are something else. This is collectively known as mimicry.

THE SIMPLEST FORM OF MIMICRY is camouflage, where an animal usually resembles its surroundings to avoid being seen by predators or prey. Many vertebrates achieve camouflage with the use of patterns and colors that help them to blend in with the background, but invertebrates are the absolute masters of disguise.

The champions of camouflage are probably a group of insects called phasmids. These are the stick and leaf insects, which resemble foliage so closely that they are almost impossible to spot unless they move. Indeed, the name phasmid is derived from the Greek *phasma*, meaning apparition or ghost. There is one obvious flaw with camouflage, however. If an animal is placed in a different habitat, it may stand out like a beacon.

A further type of mimicry works on the basis that there are species to be mimicked that are harmful to potential predators. The mimic therefore enjoys immunity from being hunted, because the predator chooses to avoid attempting to eat it.

Hoverfly
This harmless fly resembles a wasp, so predators may choose to avoid eating it for fear of being stung.

Cretan bee orchid
In the case of this flower, looking like a bee serves to attract real bees, which fertilize it with pollen in their attempts to mate.

There are different types of mimicry, but one of the most basic types is called "Batesian mimicry," after English naturalist, Henry Bates (1825–92) who first described the practice whereby a harmless species is protected by resemblance to another species that is harmful to a predator.

A German naturalist, Johann F.T. Müller (1821–97), described a more complex type of mimicry where several harmful species share the benefits of resembling each other. This is called "Müllerian mimicry" in his honor.

The classic examples of this are species of insect that mimic the warning coloration of wasps and hornets. This arrangement of black and yellow stripes can be seen in species of moth, beetle, and fly that are perfectly harmless to a predator such as a bird. The deception works, however, because birds learn from experience that black and yellow stripes usually come with a nasty sting.

Sri Lankan cricket
This is one of many insects that seek to camouflage themselves from predatory eyes by mimicking the appearance of leaves.

© DIAGRAM

Million years ago	Events
5,000–4,000	4,550 Formation of the Earth
4,000–3,000	3,800 First terrestrial rocks
	3,600 Origins of life
	3,200 First cyanobacteria
3,000–1,000	2,600 Main diversity of bacteria in existence
	2,500 Start of modern plate tectonics and continental drift; existence of free oxygen in the atmosphere
	2,400 First organisms with a cell nucleus
Organism	1,400 First multicellular organisms
1,000–500	1,000 Existence of photosynthesizing algae
	560 First multicellular animals forming communities in the sea
Multicellular animal	545 Explosion of life in shallow seas; first shelled animals
	540 First trilobites
500–400	490 Life spreads to the open ocean
	475 First corals and moss animals
	465 First jawless fish
	455 First land plants
	440 First jawed fish; first placoderm fish
Jawless fish	417 First land animals
400–300	390 First ferns; first seed-bearing plants
	365 First gymnosperm plants
	360 First "amphibians"
Early amphibian	325 First reptiles
300–100	300 First flying insects
	250 Extinction of trilobites
	230 First dinosaurs
	210 First mammals
	150 First birds
Flying insect	140 First flowering plants
100–now	100 First primates
	65 Extinction of ammonites and dinosaurs
	55 Mammals diversified
	4 First hominids

Fossils help scientists determine when different kinds of plants and animals first appeared.

Era	Millions of years ago	Period	Main events
Proterozoic Eon	2,500–543	Proterozoic periods	bacteria, simple animals, and plants exist
Paleozoic	543–490	Cambrian	sea animals without a backbone flourish
	490–443	Ordovician	early fish appear
	443–417	Silurian	land plants and land arthropods appear
	417–354	Devonian	insects and amphibians appear
	354–290	Carboniferous	reptiles and flying insects live in forests
	290–248	Permian	reptiles dominate
Mesozoic	248–206	Triassic	dinosaurs dominate, mammals appear
	206–144	Jurassic	birds appear and pterosaurs flourish
	144–65	Cretaceous	flowering plants appear
Cenozoic	65–1.8	Tertiary	dinosaurs die out, mammals spread
	1.8–present	Quaternary	humans dominate

© DIAGRAM

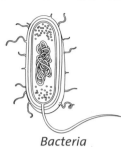

Bacteria

Bacteriophage

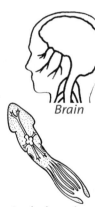

Brain

Cephalopod

Crustacean

adaptation The change that results when a species has to cope with a new or altering environment.

amino acid A simple organic compound comprising the elements carbon, hydrogen, nitrogen, and oxygen.

ammonite An extinct form of cephalopod that lived in a coiled and buoyant shell.

amphibian A semi-aquatic animal that relies on water as a habitat for its egg and larval stages, but can survive on land as an adult.

angiosperms Plants that produce seeds contained in an ovary.

animal An organism that can typically respond quickly in reaction to stimuli, is generally mobile by nature, and feeds on organic matter.

arachnid A terrestrial arthropod, characterized by having two body parts (cephalothorax and abdomen), four pairs of legs, and one pair of appendages called palps.

arthropod An animal with an exoskeleton and jointed limbs and body.

bacteria (singular: **bacterium**) Single-celled microorganisms that lack a cell nucleus.

bacteriophage A virus that preys upon bacteria and multiplies by taking over their cellular substances.

blood The fluid medium that circulates around an animal's body, delivering and removing chemicals as necessary.

brain The hub of the nervous system in animals, where nerve impulses are interpreted and reactions are decided upon.

calcium carbonate ($CaCO_3$) The white, brittle substance in shells and bones.

carbon dioxide (CO_2) A colorless and odorless compound gas emitted as a waste product of respiration in animals, but essential for photosynthesis in plants.

cellulose The fibrous substance in the cell walls of plants—a complex sugar molecule.

cephalopod A squid, octopus, or related invertebrate.

characteristic A particular feature of an animal or plant.

chitin The tough substance in the exoskeletons of arthropods.

chlorophyll The greenish chemical in typical plants, which produces food by the process of photosynthesis.

cladistics Classification of animals by their presumed evolutionary relationships.

collagen The rubbery substance in animal cell walls and bones—a protein.

compound A substance made of chemically combined elements.

convergent evolution Where unrelated organisms evolved similarities reflecting similar lifestyles.

crustacean An aquatic or terrestrial arthropod typically with head, thorax, segmented abdomen, five pairs of legs, and one pair of appendages adapted as claws.

cyanobacteria (singular: **cyanobacterium**) Blue-green bacteria with chlorophyll for photosynthesis.

cytoplasm The nonnuclear substance of a cell, where its proteins are made and life processes occur.

dicotyledons Flowering plants (**angiosperms**) with two seed leaves.

DNA (deoxyribonucleic acid) The organic molecule that carries the genetic code for making living things.

ecosystem The animals, plants, and other organisms that form an interactive community with their physical surroundings.

egg A reproductive cell produced by a female.

endoskeleton An internal skeleton or framework.

environment The wider surroundings of an animal or plant—for instance, vegetation, landforms, and climate.

eukaryotes All life-forms except bacteria and Archaea. Unlike them, eukaryotes have a cell nucleus.

evolution The process of gradual change by which one type of living thing gives rise to another.

exoskeleton An external skeleton or framework.

fossil The remains or traces of an ancient organism, preserved in rocks by the geological process of fossilization.

ganglion (plural: **ganglia**). A junction of nerve fibers in animals. A brain is a complex of differently specialized ganglia.

genes A short section of the DNA of a chromosome in a cell nucleus. Genes determine inherited characteristics.

gymnosperms Nonflowering seed-bearing plants including coniferous trees such as firs and spruces.

habitat The immediate surroundings of an animal or plant, for example a river or forest.

insect An arthropod invertebrate, characterized by having three body parts—head, thorax, abdomen—three pairs of legs, and typically living terrestrially.

invertebrate Animals without a backbone, although some have a spinal cord.

larva (plural: **larvae**). The intermediate form of an animal—invertebrate or primitive vertebrate—that develops between the egg and adult forms.

living fossil A term used to describe a living plant or animal that has changed little since the time when its kind first evolved.

marsupial One of the group of mammals that gives birth to very immature young, which are then kept in a pouch of skin on the mother for a while.

metazoans All multicelled animals, including, corals, worms, mollusks, crustaceans, arachnids, insects, fish, amphibians, reptiles, birds, and mammals.

mineral A substance that is not of organic origin, but derived from the rocks that make up the Earth's crust.

molecule A group of atoms bonded together and able to take part in a chemical reaction.

monocotyledons Angiosperm plants that produce seeds with just one leaf.

natural selection The process in nature favoring the survival of those individuals best adapted to their environment, and so with the best chance of passing on their genes.

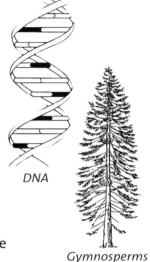

DNA

Gymnosperms

Insect

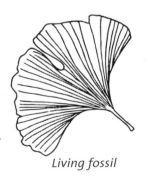

Living fossil

Marsupial mammals

©DIAGRAM

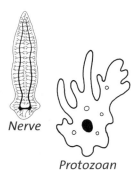

Nerve

Protozoan

Photosynthesis

Symbiotic relationship

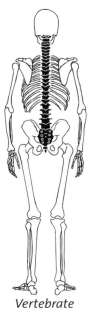

Vertebrate

nerve A bundle of elongated cells conducting electric signals and forming part of an animal's nervous system.

nucleus A self-contained bundle of genetic information (chromosomes) within the cell of an animal or plant.

organic A substance derived from an animal or plant.

organism Any life-form—plant, animal, or bacterium.

oxygen (O) A colorless and odorless gas emitted by plants as a waste product of photosynthesis, but essential for respiration in animals.

parasitic relationship A lifestyle in which one organism benefits at the expense of another.

parazoans Multicelled animals lacking defined body parts.

photosynthesis The process by which plants use light energy to help them make food.

placental mammals Mammals whose unborn young are nourished in the mother's womb by an organ called a placenta.

prion A suborganism even more basic than a virus, but difficult to destroy because it is not alive in the true sense of the word.

prokaryotes Single-celled life-forms without distinct nuclei—bacteria and Archaea.

protein An organic compound made from strings of amino acids.

protozoan A single-celled animal-like eukaryote.

respiration The chemical process by which animals derive energy from food. It is loosely used to mean breathing.

sap The fluid medium that flows within plants, carrying chemicals from the roots to the leaves (xylem sap), and from leaves to the rest of the plant (phloem sap).

seed A protected package containing the genetic information necessary to create a plant and supplied with a food source to aid initial growth.

spore The package of genetic information necessary to create a plant such as a fern or moss, but lacking the protective casing and food source of seeds.

suborganisms The most primitive of life-forms—viruses, prions, and virinos—that can survive only inside the cells of host organisms.

symbiotic relationship A lifestyle in which two organisms benefit more or less equally from a partnership.

taxonomy The scientific classification of organisms.

vertebrae The tubular bones that make up the spine in vertebrate animals and carry the spinal cord.

vertebrate Animals with a backbone, made from vertebrae.

virino The form a prion takes when it is active within the cell of a host organism.

virus A suborganism only able to survive within the cells of an animal or plant because it lacks the components necessary to be self-supporting.

There is a lot of useful information on the internet. There are also many sites that are fun to use. Remember that you may be able to get information on a particular topic by using a search engine such as Google (*http://www.google.com*). Some of the sites that are found in this way may be very useful, others not. Below is a selection of websites related to the material covered by this book. Most are illustrated, and they are mainly of the type that provides useful facts.

Facts On File, Inc. *takes no responsibility for the information contained within these websites. All the sites were accessible as of September 1, 2003.*

BBC Education: Evolution
An educational site from the British Broadcasting Corporation, with details of its "Life On Earth" television series.
http://www.bbc.co.uk/education/darwin/loe/

Biology Online
An investigation of the origins of life and how it has evolved over geological periods.
http://www.biology-online.org/tutorials/9_evolution_origins.htm

Geological Survey: Learning Web
An educational site exploring the Earth, including rocks and minerals, land, water, and living things. Specifically for K-12 age groups.
http://www.usgs.gov/education/

Missouri Association for Creation: The Genesis Network
Creationist perspectives on the origins of life.
http://www.gennet.org

Museum Victoria: Prehistoric Life
A good summary of the anatomy and fossil history of many groups of invertebrates.
http://www.museum.vic.gov.au/prehistoric/time/

Nature
Science news from the online journal.
http://www.nature.com

New Scientist
Online news from the world of science, including discoveries and controversies in paleontology.
http://www.newscientist.com

Open Directory Project: Evolution
A comprehensive listing of internet resources.
http://dmoz.org/Science/Biology/Evolution/

San Diego State University: Evolution of Life on Earth
A chemist's view of evolution, with comparisons of scientific and creationist views.
http://www.scibridge.sdsu.edu/coursemats/introsci/evolution/evolution_of_life.html

Scientific American
News from the world of science and technology.
http://www.sciam.com

Stephen Jay Gould Website
A website devoted to the acclaimed biological theorist, with links to many of his articles.
http://www.stephenjaygould.org

Tree of Life Web Project
The site of the Tree of Life, which provides information about the diversity of organisms on the Earth, their history, and characteristics.
http://tolweb.org/tree/phylogeny.html

UCB, Museum of Paleontology: Evolution
A rich source of information about evolution and the evolution–creation controversy.
http://www.ucmp.berkeley.edu/history/evolution.html

UCB, Museum of Paleontology: Introduction to Cladistics
An introduction to the modern method of classifying living organisms.
http://www.ucmp.berkeley.edu/clad/clad1.html

UCB, Museum of Paleontology: Vendian Animals
Photographs of and information about some of the earliest animal fossils. The site includes links to other groups and other periods of the Earth's history.
http://www.ucmp.berkeley.edu/vendian/critters.html

University of Texas, McDonald Observatory: Stardate
A detailed survey of the Earth, including geography, geology, tides, climate, and exploration.
http://stardate.org/resources/ssguide/earth.html

World Atlas of Biodiversity
Excellent interactive maps of the world's flora and fauna.
http://stort.unep-wcmc.org/imaps/gb2002/book/viewer.htm